To. Geoff

D0863206

Thanks for your
Support 9 Sept 2010
thanks

Allen Hunt

Buffalo Soldier

What My Country
Did For Me

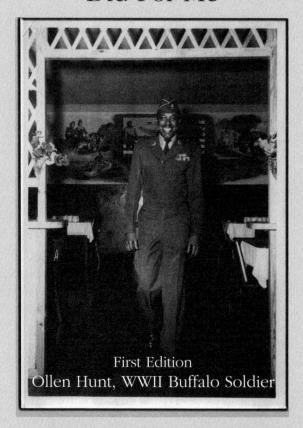

First Edition
Ollen Hunt, WWII Buffalo Soldier

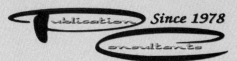

Publication Since 1978
Consultants

PO Box 221974 Anchorage, Alaska 99522-1974

ISBN 978-1-59433-044-5

Library of Congress Catalog Card Number: 2006903545

Manufactured in the United States of America.

Acknowledgements

No book would be complete without recognition of those who made the book possible. I would like to thank my parents, my wife, my children, and other family members for their guidance and support through the years. I would like to thank the United States Government and the Armed Forces for the training and life experiences they have provided to me. To the men and women who served with me in World War II, thank you for the memories. It was an honor to serve by your side.

Thank you to Northwest Airlines for their willingness to hire a retired veteran and to all the friends and employees who worked with me in my businesses in Alaska—the Hof Brau, J.C. Penney's Coffee Shop, The Iron Gate, and The Sandwich Deck.

Thank you to my friends at Anchorage Cold Storage for their friendship and support over the years.

Thank you to Joanne Rinker and Betty Meyer for their long hours in the drafting and typing of this book.

Thank you.

Contents

Foreword
by Steven Stover

I have known Ollen Hunt for twenty years or so and proud to say so. The Hof Brau Restaurant that he ran served excellent food, especially the prime rib, which was widely held as the largest portions in town. The Red Baron Lounge right next door to the Hof Brau was a melting pot of regulars to include white, Native, and black patrons, most of them veterans, which is a testament to Ollen's colorblind outlook on life. Ollen never discriminated against anyone. He was especially kind to Alaska Natives, hiring many. During the Alaska Federation of Natives Convention they all came to his restaurant. The police had several banquets at the Hof Brau as well. People just felt comfortable there.

Ollen's extensive time spent overseas educated him in life experiences about people. I will forever remember Ollen behind the serving line at the Hof Brau, white chef hat on, carving prime rib for people as diverse as welfare mothers to Supreme Court Justices who would sit down at tables covered with long red tablecloths and enjoy their meal.

Anchorage has lost a little compassion, equality, and leadership since the closing of the Hof Brau, Red Baron, and miniature Bus Stop. The world would be a better place with more Ollen Hunts in it. Ollen has been an inspiration to me and many others. We wouldn't be surprised if he opened up another restaurant someday, somewhere. Let's hope so!

Ollen's Friend,
Steven Stover

Introduction

I am writing this book to share with the reader my personal "lifetime of learning." It follows my life from its beginnings on a farm in Tennessee, through the barracks in the Civilian Conservation Corps (CCC), to the foxholes in the Serchio Valley and the Apennine Mountains of Italy during World War II, and on to the wilderness of Alaska.

In my eighty-plus years I have met people from all walks of life from all over the world in my service to my country. In this book I remember the people, the places, the opportunities:

- Training and education passed on to me by my mother and father
- Experience and education I received in the Civilian Conservation Corps
- Post-World War II assignment and experience in France, England, and Germany
- Return to the United States in 1957, and my assignment to Fort Lewis, Washington
- Retirement in 1963 after twenty-one years in military service
- Assignment to Anchorage, Alaska by Northwest Airlines, and the start of my own business in downtown Anchorage about six years later—the first of five businesses (four restaurants and a clothing store)
- Companies that assisted me in my business ventures
- Organizations for which I served on Boards of Directors

Long before President Kennedy said, "Ask not what your country can do for you—ask what you can do for your country," I had asked myself that question.

I thank God for his protection and guidance through this lifetime of learning.

The town of McLemoresville, was founded around 1820 and is located in Carroll County, Tennessee, about 9 miles west of Huntingdon. Carroll County lies on the dividing ridge between the Tennessee and the Mississippi rivers. The county was first organized in McLemoresville. Before the advent of the railroads, McLemoresville was an important place of commerce.

The Black Church has no challenger as the cultural womb of the black community. Not only did it give birth to new institutions such as schools, banks, insurance companies, and low-income housing, it also provided an academy and an arena for political activities, and it nurtured young talent for musical, dramatic, and artistic development. E. Franklin Frazier's apt descriptive phrase, "nation within a nation," pointed to these multifarious levels of community involvement found in the Black Church, in addition to the traditional concerns of worship, moral nurture, education, and social control. Much of black culture is heavily indebted to the black religious tradition, including most forms of black music, drama, literature, storytelling, and even humor.

C. Eric Lincoln and Lawrence H. Mamiya, 1990

Part One
Childhood

Chapter 1
Family Life

My mother, Mattie V. Frame, was a widow with two children and a farm. My father, Sant Hunt, was a widower with seven children and a farm. I don't know any of the particulars, but they met and married.

We may not have been the only black family in the state of Tennessee with two farms, but I doubt if there were many others.

Older siblings are blurred in my memory. Some left home before I was born or old enough to relate to them. Their names were Eather Hunt, Wilbert Hunt, Colier Hunt, Curlie Hunt, Dola Hunt, Maude Hunt, Trever Hunt, Wasteller Frame, Connie Mae Frame, and Ivy Nell Hunt. My father's oldest son died in infancy. Another married son lived nearby with his family.

One sister, Dola, married and left home when I was about six years old. Sometime later, she moved back. At the time, I gave it no thought. I have since wondered why Dola, a practicing Baptist and a believer in "until death do us part," left her husband. What terrible event drove her to it remains a family secret. She eventually left home again when she married a preacher.

Mama and Papa had two children. My sister Ivy Nell was born in 1921. I arrived on July 25, 1923, making a total of eleven children from the combined families, although there were never more than six living at home at any one time.

We were brothers and sisters, all of us. Mama told us over and over again, "There are no half sisters or brothers, no stepsisters or brothers in our home," she said. "Everyone is equal to everyone else, and must respect each other."

About once a month Mama and Papa held a family meeting after supper was eaten and our homework was done. We sat around the big fireplace in the dining room. Every meeting began the same way, with either Mama or Papa saying "Everyone is created by God. God controls this earth and everything on it. He created all types of food for every living creature on this earth. He gave us the knowledge to prepare the food for consumption. He gave us all other things used by mankind. You may find that different people have different ways of preparing items, but that knowledge is given to all of us by God."

They would also say, "Remember this: No matter who you meet, or what country they are from, rich or poor, what color they are—white or black, or whatever—we are all the same. Everyone is a human being created by God. They are no better than you are and you are no better than they are. You treat everyone as a human being created by God.

"On this earth we have rules and laws. You are to obey them. You must all respect each other," Mama would say. "You must treat everyone else the way you want to be treated. Everyone is your equal and must be treated as such. If everyone does this, everyone will get along with each other."

She went on to say that this rule didn't just apply to our immediate family. We must respect everyone, white and black, old and young alike.

Then Mama and Papa brought up things they thought were important for us to know. They told us what was expected of us. They pointed out what our responsibilities were—to family, church and community. It was in these family meetings that the groundwork for my future began—my desire to serve my fellow man and ultimately, my country.

Their instructions and teachings were heeded by all of us. I cannot remember even one instance when any of us children had an argument.

———

I was the baby of the family. Everyone spoiled me. Sometimes two sisters wanted to hold me at the same time. Or the girls wanted me to sit between them on the porch swing and my brother wanted me to play with him in the yard. I had the deciding vote.

I trailed after my big brothers and sisters all over the farm.

They liked having me along. If I got tired, one of them carried me on their back. There didn't seem to be any disadvantages to being the youngest member of the family.

I tagged along when the boys did their chores. As soon as I was big enough, my brothers gave me a stick or two of kindling to carry, while they took the heavy wood indoors to fuel the cook stove and fireplace. My parents made a big thing of how much help I was.

"We can't start a fire without kindling," Mama said.

"Ollen's a worker," Papa said. "Pretty soon he'll be carrying firewood."

I sure was proud of myself when I was able to bring in an arm load of wood. I knew how important it was.

———

As I grew, my chores included feeding livestock and milking cows. Milking was not my favorite chore.

I didn't mind feeding the animals. The cows were docile. They stood still as long as I'd rub their faces just above their eyes. Papa said it was because it kept flies away. The horses would give their heads a hard shake when flies were too bothersome. The long mane on top of their heads and down their necks swished back and forth, like a built-in flyswatter. When it was time to head to the barn for their evening feed, I could get a fast ride to the barn, my legs sticking straight out on either side.

Our pigs were another story. They weren't that much trouble unless they managed to get out of their pen. But they wallowed in any mud they could find, even their own manure. They smelled terrible. And squeal! They seemed to know when I was heading their way with feed or water and tried to out-squeal each other. We fed, watered, and tolerated them until butchering time came. Then it was ham and salt pork for another winter.

Like every other farm family, we had chickens. Fresh eggs made a good breakfast. And the stuff Mama baked with eggs tasted wonderful.

But chickens, I discovered, aren't very nice. They peck in dirt and dung. They peck each other. When they get provoked—and it doesn't take much to provoke a hen wanting to hatch her eggs—they peck people.

The girls would wrap aprons or skirts around their arms, sneak close, reach under a hen, and grab the eggs and run, hoping to escape an ever ready sharp beak. It never worked, but as long as they kept their faces averted and their arms covered, they didn't fare too badly. Occasionally, a hen jumped from the nest squawking, puffed her feathers out and gave chase.

Chickens have pecked me. They have flapped me with their outstretched wings and that packs a nasty wallop. When I was small, I considered egg gathering a dangerous and dreaded chore.

There is not much good I can say about chickens. Probably the best thing about a chicken is looking at the pile of bones left on the plate after it's been eaten.

Farm chores were pretty evenly divided between women-folks and menfolks, but there was always overlap if someone was ill or away. Sometimes I had to fill the oil lamps in the evening or one of the girls might help carry in wood.

Hauling water was everybody's job. We had a dug well and used what was called a pull bucket to get the water. To crank down the empty bucket was easy. It was hard work pulling it up filled with five gallons of water. Mama some-times remarked she was glad our well had a barrier around it so the water stayed clean and we couldn't fall in it.

In those days, there was no indoor plumbing. We bathed in the washtub and used lots of water for laundry, cooking, and canning as well. It seemed like there was always some-one coming or going with a water bucket.

Another family chore was Mama's large vegetable garden behind the house. We raised cabbage, kohlrabi, lettuce, Brus-sels sprouts, kale, turnips, parsnips, tomatoes of all kinds, several kinds of squash, peas, beans of various varieties, radishes, onions, watermelons, muskmelons, carrots, beets, pumpkins—just about any vegetable you can think of.

There were separate potato, corn, and strawberry patches. We knew when Papa sold the surplus we'd get new school clothes; maybe even a treat.

Many evenings the entire family spent an hour or two weeding so Mama could can and store plenty of vegetables for winter. Then we'd sit on the porch and have some of Mama's good lemonade with ice chips in it from the big block in the icebox.

The telephone system in those days was not like it is today. Those were party-line days. Our call was two long rings and one short ring. The telephone was reserved for matters of importance, so it didn't ring often.

My father chewed tobacco. He used a spittoon. I think every family I knew had a spittoon. He occasionally smoked a pipe in the evenings, sitting in what we called his "chief" chair, because it was the biggest chair we had and he was the only one that sat in it.

He made home brew too, and kept it in the smokehouse. When people came to visit, he'd inevitably take the men there. They had a drink or two, then came back and sat on the porch to talk. None of them ever overindulged, including my father. And he never brought the home brew out of the smokehouse, not even to the porch.

We children were not allowed to go to the smokehouse. We were nearing adulthood before we knew why. It didn't occur to us to question the restriction or wonder why Papa took his friends there. Farmers often went to barns or outbuildings to talk.

Two of my older brothers once sneaked some booze in the house. Mama found it, poured it out and laid down the law. They didn't repeat their mistake. My mother never allowed alcohol in the house.

None of us took up chewing tobacco. I'm sure that pleased her, as it wasn't uncommon for a man to misjudge the distance to the spittoon.

I was six years old in 1929 when the stock market crashed. We still ate three meals a day and had a place to sleep. Nothing changed on the farm. When I went to school, wages were low and money wasn't flowing, but that affected everybody—white and black alike. We raised most of our food. Sometimes my brothers worked a couple of days for pay. When there was something special my father asked one of us kids to do, he gave us a little money. Sometimes our neighbor, Ed Rogers, had us help him and he'd pay us. It was never much, but we were glad to earn it.

Being a young child, I didn't have a realistic idea about the value of money, but one day I learned a particularly important lesson about it and it stayed with me for the rest of my life.

When I was about nine, Mama sent me to the store to get sugar. I rode the horse to town to buy the sugar, a distance of about three miles. There was some change, so I bought candy with it. I knew I wasn't supposed to, but I figured I could get away with it. I told Mama I didn't get any change—so not only did I take the money, but, even worse, I also lied to her. She knew how much sugar cost and how much change there would be. She gave me three chances to change my story. When I didn't, she got Papa's razor strap and gave me my due.

"I'll raise you right or I'll kill you," she said. "You stole money from your own father. If you would steal from your father, you would steal from anyone."

Since then, I've handled huge sums of money, but I've never touched a penny that didn't belong to me. Mama gave me a lesson in honesty I never forgot.

My father came home one evening from a nearby general store. It was a place where a bunch of black guys would sit around and talk. If the storekeeper wasn't busy he sat and chatted with them. One guy, thinking he was clever, had his britches legs tied shut with twine. He put quite a bit of stuff in his pants leg. When he was leaving the store, one of the strings came loose and all of it fell on the floor. The owner told him, "I'm not going to call the police, but I want you to take this mop and mop this whole store and we'll call it a day." I thought he got off easier than I did, but I finally realized having everyone know you're a thief is worse than a beating.

Chapter 2
Church Influence

We went to the Baptist Church, and we dressed up. Everyone did. During the week, Papa wore overalls and Mama wore cotton dresses. Women didn't wear pants in those days. Children wore what we called "everyday clothes." But on Sunday, that all changed.

Papa wore a suit, white shirt, tie, and a hat. He removed the hat before entering the church, out of respect. The women kept their hats on in church. I liked to look at Mama when she wore her church dress and hat.

We liked to dress up, too. My sisters always hoped they'd look a bit more stylish than the other girls. My brothers and I compared how we looked to the other boys. We'd punch each other in the ribs. "Do I look sharper than he does?" we'd whisper.

We always had dress pants, a white shirt, and a hat. I wanted a suit so I'd outshine the other boys. When I was about seven, my father had one made for me, against my mother's wishes.

"Ollen's growing so fast, he'll outgrow it in no time," she said. "And money is hard to come by." Depression or no Depression, I was the sharpest-looking boy in church until the suit became too small.

I was my father's pride and joy. I heard Mama say so. But that didn't mean I got away with anything. I noticed some of the boys wore their caps tilted a little to the side to look sharp. Before I could even think of trying it in front of the mirror at home, Papa brought it up. He thought it was disrespectful.

"Ollen," he warned. "If you don't wear your cap straight, I'll knock it off your head."

When my parents left church on Sunday, they took their Christianity with them. At night, either Mama or Papa read to us from the Bible. They stressed a life of service to others and they lived it every day—service to each other, family, friends and neighbors.

They were always willing to help a stranger as well. They considered it all as part of their service to God. We lived too far from the railroad for any hobos to come our way, but if any had, Mama would have fed them.

A horse and buggy was our transportation for a long time. Finally, Papa bought a new Ford, so one of my brothers could drive us to church and wherever else we needed to go. Several families bought new Fords about the same time so we didn't feel conspicuous.

Mama's faith guided and encouraged me to the Mourner's Bench. That was a bench at the front of the church reserved for those who had not yet accepted a religious belief. It was mostly occupied by young people, but at times older people sat there, too. The congregation prayed for them.

I must have been about twelve when I occupied the Mourner's Bench. When I had faith in my heart that it would be right for me to join the church and to try to live up to its Christian precepts, I told my parents and the preacher.

After I was baptized in a nearby river, I became a member of the church. There were lots of "Amens!" "Hallelujahs!" and "Praise Gods!" from the congregation.

Mama sang in the choir. When Baptists sing, they raise their arms to heaven and sometimes shout. It is spontaneous, a joyous worship of the Lord.

I have never forgotten what I learned in that church. The teachings have helped guide me through life.

When I got to be a teenager, a lot of my friends were either not going to church or sneaking out after the services started when their mothers wouldn't notice. They wanted me to sneak out with them. I might have been tempted, but Mama sang in the choir and frequently looked over to see if her children were sitting quietly and paying attention. I stayed put. I knew what would happen if Mama noticed I was gone.

The two most important influences in my life have always

been family and church. The family meetings and instructions have guided me, whatever part of the world I was in. The advice my parents gave me has worked in both military and civilian life.

My brothers and sisters also followed our parents' rules. They have all been successful, too.

Our parents guided us by example and instruction. If we did wrong, we were disciplined, but we always knew our parents loved us.

My successes in life are the result of my parents' guidance. It's a debt I could never repay.

Chapter 3
Racism

A white family, the Rogers, lived nearby. We got to know them well. Ed Rogers and Papa traded work when another pair of hands was needed. Mama and Mrs. Rogers traded recipes. We played with their kids. Sometimes we all had Sunday dinners at our house and sometimes at theirs. While the adults talked about whatever interested them we played ball out back.

I had no idea that in much of the South such interaction between whites and blacks would not have been tolerated. Ed Rogers once remarked to Papa that he didn't give a damn what other people thought; he'd be a friend with whomever he pleased.

When Ed's wife died, he sent a car to pick up my parents and take them to the funeral. And years after I left Tennessee, Ed's son still asked about me whenever he saw my dad. People were friendly. Whites and blacks lived side by side, with neighbor helping neighbor.

One of my brothers lived next door to a white family. The husband came over one evening while I was there. The two had a couple of drinks together while they talked. It didn't strike me as anything out of the ordinary. It was many years before I realized how remarkable my childhood was. Racism was something I was never aware of. And although I found out later that it was a fact of life and law in the South, I don't remember ever hearing the word *segregation*. Inequality and discrimination were foreign words to me.

When I got older, if I took a bus from one town to another, I sat where I chose to and often shared a seat with a white person. It seemed in our little corner of Tennessee there were no race problems.

If anyone had damage to their buildings from a fire or storm, the churches, both black and white, took up a collection and the whole community turned out to rebuild or repair the damage.

For instance, when one black family lost a barn everybody pitched in to help. The preacher's wife from the white Methodist Church didn't look at the color of a man's skin before she handed him a plate full of food at noon. All the women worked together, cooking and serving the men. The men worked together to rebuild the barn. Race had nothing to do with it. It was the same when a white church lost most of its roof in a storm.

One of my few childhood remembrances of anything pertaining to racial discrimination was when the nearby town of Trezevant placed four toilets at the train station—one for black women, one for black men, one for white women and one for white men. There were people in the community who rose up to speak out against those arrangements. Two of the restrooms were removed and the remaining two were simply marked "women" and "men."

Although we went to separate churches and separate schools, as a youngster I assumed that was by preference. It did not occur to me that anyone would care where I went to school or which church I attended. I didn't see a problem, and anyway, I was happy with the arrangement. I had lots of black *and* white friends and we found plenty of time to do things together.

In some ways our area was typical of the rural South at that time; white farmers and black farmers alike were cash poor. We knew we were all in the same boat, and this may have contributed to the strong sense of community I saw regularly practiced by the people of McLemoresville. Our roomy four-bedroom house was comparable to other homes, maybe better than some.

I was probably in the third grade when the local white banker hired me to come in once a week after school and sweep the bank floors. I took my job seriously and swept the floors as clean as I could, for which I earned a small sum. Occasionally, he had me sit in his big swivel chair, then called the staff into his office.

"Look here," he'd say. "Look who's the boss now!" Everyone laughed, especially the banker. It must have been pretty amusing for them to see a small black boy sitting in a chair that a black man had no opportunity to occupy. Being too young to be concerned with understanding their amusement, I was pleased to think the banker liked me well enough to pretend I could do his job. And I just liked being the center of attention.

Part Two
Beginning My Lifetime of Learning

Chapter 4
School Years

When I turned five, Mama said she was going to teach me about school. There was no kindergarten or preschool or day care back then. Children entered first grade at age six or seven, having learned whatever their parents chose to teach them, or had the time to teach them.

The year before, when Mama coached Ivy Nell in the ABCs, I listened and repeated to myself what I could remember. I learned a little bit about numbers, too. All during Ivy Nell's first grade school year, I hung around while Mama went over her lessons with her. I picked up quite a bit.

Every member of my family except me had been to school, and I wanted to go. Now it was my turn. I paid attention to everything Mama said. I repeated the alphabet over and over, until she was satisfied that I knew it. I learned some of my numbers, too. I listened when Mama read to me and tried to figure out the words on the page.

My sisters liked to play school. Of course, they were always "the teacher," but that was okay with me—I liked being the student.

Papa taught me to tie my shoelaces. He showed me how to tie them tight so they wouldn't come untied. At that time, Velcro fasteners were unheard of.

To prepare me for school, Mama drilled me on everything she could think of:

Listen to the teacher.
Be nice to the other students.
Wait your turn.
Pay attention.

Dress neat and clean.
Sit up straight.
Do not talk in class.
Raise your hand if you have a question.

My mother went with me to Dunbar School the first two days. Other mothers went with their first-graders too. The school was all black, both students and teachers. My teacher was nice, but strict. The school had four large classrooms with sliding doors so the rooms could be made larger or smaller. We had outside well water and outside toilets. There were wood stoves for heating and cooking. Some kids drank from the communal dipper and some had cups of their own.

I felt good about going to school because my mother had taught me so much. My brothers and sisters had talked to me a lot about school. They were always saying, "Be smart and you can be anything you want to be." I didn't know what I wanted to be but I knew I wanted to be smart. Ivy Nell was one grade ahead of me. As we went forward I learned a lot from her.

———

Each of the teachers taught more than one grade. There were four rooms for the eight grades. Most of the time each teacher taught two grades. That seemed to work out pretty well.

The parents took turns cooking at the school so we had a hot lunch every day. They also brought in loads of firewood for heat and cooking. It was really a community effort that kept the school going, unheard of in most schools in the '30s—white or black.

Some time after I started school, a group of black women got together and started a kindergarten in a home. The only thing the government had in it was that they had to give their approval. They didn't put out any money, though.

It didn't affect me, but it has been one more reason for me to reflect on what a progressive community I lived in at the time.

———

We addressed our teachers as "ma'am" and "sir," having been taught by our parents to respect them. There were few discipline problems and those few were minor. If a couple of boys began to argue on the playground, their teacher was almost sure to take their recess away from them. While everyone else was outside having fun, they sat at their desks and did whatever the teacher gave them to do.

Repeat offenders might get a spanking and someone from the school would call the parents. It was almost certain they'd get another whipping when they got home.

The whole community system worked to keep kids in line and I can't recall anyone ever getting expelled. If neighbors or teachers saw a child doing wrong, they stopped them, and then informed the parents. On rare occasions, if the wrongdoing merited it, they might administer something more than words, and then call the parents. I never heard of parents getting angry with a neighbor for chastising their children. A child with a reputation for being a troublemaker would have no friends. Parents would not allow their children to associate with a "bad apple." That was drilled into us, over and over.

In fact, my father used to say, "If you don't follow the rules, when the judge is finished, I'm going to be rougher than the judge." Needless to say, I did my best to stay out of trouble, as did the rest of the kids.

———

I enjoyed school. As I passed from one grade to the next, I was always ready to learn whatever the teacher had to teach me.

We had recess, both morning and afternoon, a period when we could go outside and play. The smaller children played on the swings and seesaws. Nearly everyone played softball.

By fifth grade, I played on the baseball and basketball teams. We played against other schools in the area. One of the teachers had a van and the school had a bus. They transported us back and forth. My parents often came to the home games.

We had many other school activities, even a fair once a year with all kinds of games and food booths. Various programs were held at night so the parents could attend, especially the plays we gave. Everybody seemed to enjoy those. We even performed the plays at other schools. I don't know if we were good actors, but we sure enjoyed performing.

Chapter 5
My Speech

In sixth grade I began to take notice of the speech contest held at the end of each school year. All seventh- and eighth-graders were required to write a speech and give it in front of the school, parents, and families. It had to be memorized. The program lasted late into the evening as student after student took their place on stage and spoke. Each speech had a topic that was uplifting and encouraging.

In the seventh and eighth grades, my sister Ivy Nell and I competed against each other. Ivy Nell took first place. I took second. I don't recall what Ivy Nell's topic was. Mine was "Don't Quit." I guess you could say I didn't, as I went back the next year determined to win.

My auntie helped me put my thoughts together. She suggested my subject, "How to Progress." We started from there. I'd come up with a statement and she'd tell me if it sounded right. I might want to use one word. She might think I should use another one. We agreed on the best word.

When it was finished, I thought it sounded good, better than any I'd heard the year before. I figured it had a pretty good chance of winning first place.

Papa helped me practice from his "chief" chair in the dining room.

"Number one, Ollen Hunt," he'd announce.

I'd walk in, head up, eyes straight ahead and go to the end of the table, my "speech spot." Sometimes Papa sent me back. "Walk a little slower," he advised, "Just a normal walk."

Papa played audience and judge. He noticed everything and commented on it. "Stand up straight, arms at your side." "Look at the audience." "Speak slower, please." "Speak louder, please." He told me to practice a pleasant expression so the judges wouldn't think I was nervous. He showed me how to present myself at the beginning of the speech, so that I looked at each group as I addressed them.

The speech contest took place in the evening. The school was filled to capacity, mostly with parents.

All the students in one grade gave their speeches. Then the other grade did the same. With so many students, it made for a long evening. There was an intermission halfway through.

In seventh grade, I had been one of the last students to speak, so I had plenty of time to compare my speech with the rest, not to mention plenty of time to get nervous. But in eighth grade, I was one of the first speakers. I was a little anxious, but I really believed I could win and I knew I looked sharp in my suit and tie.

When my name was called, I did exactly what Papa had drilled into me. I stepped up onto the stage and walked to the center. Then I took a deep breath and delivered my speech, just as I had done so many times at home.

When my speech was over. I took another deep breath. "Thank you," I said, and then bowed, as Papa had instructed me. I walked off the stage to a lot of applause.

The evening dragged on as student after student gave speech after speech. As I listened to each, I compared them to what I had said and wondered—what would the judges decide?

I won! I was presented with an award, a letter, and a trophy. The excitement of winning the contest stayed with me for a long time after, and the words of my speech have stayed with me ever since. I have shared it with many people and I've tried to live up to it. This is my speech, exactly as I gave it.

How to Progress

Honorable judges, members of the faculty, student body, ladies and gentlemen, strangers and friends-to-be.

My subject tonight is How to Progress. I wonder as you sit in your place and indulge us—are you trying to do something toward helping others? Are you trying to keep things still? Don't give up. Because the man who takes more interest in the things around him is the one the world looks up to today.

My friends, God shows little children humanity. He wants young men and women who are able and strong. It is not enough to say that we believe in God. We must all build our lives and have faith.

If you wish to progress, you must aim higher than you can strike because the man who doesn't reach his ambition has aimed at some lower point.

If you are a doctor, be the best doctor. Even if you are a neighbor, be the best neighbor.

Young men and women, love the truth. Follow the right path for the sake of right.

Build your foundation so firm that in your later life if you are shaken you will not fall. Progress is won by fighting, not by regular force, but with the brain.

The Bible says as a man is thinking so is he, and I believe that. If you think that you will win, you will win. If you think that you will lose, you have lost.

Progress and success begin with us. It is all in the state of mind. Life's battle doesn't always go to the strongest or fastest man.

The man who wins is the man who thinks he can.

A week later, I graduated from eighth grade. My parents beamed from the audience as I walked on stage and received my diploma. It was another proud moment for all of us. It also marked the end of one era of my life and the beginning of another. I had finished my formal education for the time being, but my learning of real life and responsibility was about to begin.

Part Three
Civilian Conservation Corps

Chapter 6
Choosing a Career

After graduating from eighth grade, I was undecided about continuing my education because there was no high school for blacks in McLemoresville. The nearest one was thirty or forty miles away and there weren't enough buses to take all who needed to go. With more students than seats, a student might not get to school every day.

My sisters walked four miles to catch the bus. They sometimes had to return home because it was already full. Both graduated, in spite of this obstacle.

I stayed on the farm, helping my parents, while trying to decide where I wanted to go to high school and college.

We had a machine to cut and rake hay, a machine to grind sorghum into juice to make molasses to sell, and other machinery geared to make farming as efficient as possible, eliminating some back-breaking labor. Still, I knew I didn't want to farm for a living.

Long before President John F. Kennedy said, "Ask not what your country can do for you: ask what you can do for your country," I had asked myself the same question. My speech stayed with me. I went over it in my mind, word by word and I decided I wanted to prepare myself to serve my country; I wanted to be of service to others. I just wasn't sure how I could go about that.

———

December was a good time for a farm boy to go to town. I didn't run into anyone I knew in McLemoresville, so I checked out the shop windows. As I turned from a display, two young guys walked toward me. They wore brown uniforms, the bright brass buttons on the jackets all neatly buttoned, pants creased so sharp my mother would have approved of them, caps set at the same jaunty angle on both

31

their heads. And their shoes—so shiny the sun bounced off them into my eyes.

It's the first time I'd seen anyone in uniform in the small town of McLemoresville. I stared. "What uniform are you wearing?" I blurted.

"We're soldiers," one said.

"We're protecting America," his buddy added.

"How can I join?" I asked

They told me where to find the recruiting office. My mind was made up. I would serve my country in the military.

It wasn't that easy. "You have to be eighteen to enlist," the recruiter told me. "Your parents can sign for you when you're seventeen."

I shook my head. "They won't."

"Then you'll have to wait."

"It's a long time to wait," I said. "I'm only fifteen and a half."

"How tall are you?"

"Six feet."

He smiled. "Well, you're tall enough. You're just not old enough. Have you considered joining the Three Cs?" he asked.

"The three seas? What's that?"

"It's a program President Roosevelt started. It stands for 'Civilian Conservation Corps.'"

"What do they do?"

"A lot of different things," he said. "They teach you a trade. You live in a barracks. There are rules and regulations you have to abide by. It's disciplined like the military."

"Do they wear uniforms?"

"They do. And you get paid. They send a check to your folks, too."

"How old do I have to be?"

"Sixteen, if your parents will sign permission."

I grinned. This might be for me. I listened to every word he said. Then I went home to try to convince my parents. I really wanted to join the CCC, but no matter how I presented it to my parents, the answer remained the same.

"No!" "No!" "No!"

Once my parents made a decision, they rarely changed their minds. It looked like I'd have a long wait before I could begin the future I had already chosen.

Chapter 7
Learning to Serve

One day I ran into a white legislator I knew. He was a man well thought of in the community, with a reputation for being helpful wherever he could. I talked to him about the Civilian Conservation Corps and about my frustration at being unable to join.

"I could learn to serve my country, just like in the military," I said.

"I think you're smart for wanting to serve your country," he said.

He offered to talk to my parents. I didn't hear their conversation, but after speaking to him, they agreed to let me join the CCC at sixteen.

The legislator drove me to a nearby town. He signed for my parents. Then I signed. He took me to an induction center where I passed the physical and became a member of the CCC.

All the new recruits were then taken to a camp, given a uniform and assigned a bed. Each day began with reveille followed by police call to clean up the area. After we finished, we returned to our barracks until someone blew a whistle signaling us to go to the mess hall for breakfast. Following breakfast we cleaned the barracks until it would pass inspection. When that was done, we were given other duties—work on roads, cleanup of the motor pool, K.P., and so forth. Recruits who had been there for a while had an assignment, but because we were new recruits, it took some time before we got ours. There were various required classes such as medical (first aid) and supply (servicing the troops—clothing, etc.) and administration. As we learned, we were able to order supplies and keep track of paperwork.

The first question I got was, "Why are you here?" It was an easy question to answer.

"To serve my country and learn a trade," I replied.

Everybody had school time. There were trades to pick from. There were food service classes as well as auto mechanics, carpentry, and construction—all kinds of classes having to do with production. I didn't have to choose a field and stay in it all the way through. I could change at any time if I didn't like what I was doing or if I thought I had learned all I needed to in that trade.

That made my decision easier. I chose cooking, a choice that marked a big change in my life.

In food service, we got up before reveille to prepare breakfast for our company. This wasn't hard for a farm boy like me. We worked in rotating shifts and worked well together in the kitchen.

If anyone created a problem, our instructor put a stop to it in short order. There was one incident where one guy hit another one in the mouth with something, breaking some teeth. The offender was discharged immediately.

There was a stockade for guys who committed severe infractions against the rules. The officers used a belt to whip those who did wrong if the supervisor thought it was an appropriate punishment. After a few guys were whipped, a lot more shaped up. At that time, it was legal to whip prisoners in the civilian jails. It wasn't considered cruel or unusual punishment.

We had an outdoor boxing ring. When a fight started, the supervisor stopped it and set a date and time to have the assailants settle their differences with boxing gloves.

—

It was six months to a year before I got home to visit. At times I got a little homesick, but they kept me pretty busy so I didn't have much time to think about home and family. I was learning a lot. It was interesting because of the variety of classes I was taking.

It marked a big change in my life when I was accepted at the food service school in Alabama. We traveled to Mumford, Alabama and were based at Fort McClellan. The government contracted for our courses and training. It was excellent training, a wonderful beginning for a great future for all those who participated.

The first step after arriving at this school was hours of discipline and instruction. Following the opening session we went to the classroom. I still remember the beginning speech in the cooking classroom.

"God made man and God made food for every creature on earth. You are here to learn to prepare food for mankind, and we will teach you how to prepare that food."

Teach us they did. We were taught to work on a definite schedule and we were given worthwhile work to do and taught how to do it. It was an interesting and enjoyable experience. I had already assisted in cooking for my company. Now I learned in depth about meal planning and preparation, food buying—everything involved in producing wholesome, healthy meals.

One of my buddies once remarked, "Ollen, you sure seem to be having a good time."

"My Mama said I might marry a girl who didn't want to cook for me or didn't know how," I told him. "She said you'd better learn to cook for yourself. That way you will always get your reward—a good meal."

Chapter 8
Foundation for the Future

My time spent in the Civilian Conservation Corps was a pleasant, satisfying learning experience. I look back on it now as the most important stepping-stone to my careers in both the public and private sector.

The CCC means many things to me. It was just a government camp to some, and merely a New Deal program to others. To some of the boys it was a place where they could spend a few months to earn money to buy a few clothes or things they had often wished for. To me, it meant a new chapter in my life and an opportunity to prepare myself for the world ahead. Having been unable to go all the way through public school as I wished, I now know that there was no better training school—vocational or academic—for making anyone a worthwhile citizen to any community than the CCC.

The CCC was a government within itself, where every law was made and enforced to ensure the greatest possible number of our rights and privileges. We were strictly protected against the antisocial. We took to heart our own duties and responsibilities to the camp and quickly became group conscious.

Discipline was strict, but obedience had its reward. Bad conduct, bad manners and temperament were smoothed by close contact with the fellows in camp. Our health was promoted by the routines and regulations of the CCC. Our food was selected for balance and prepared so we were the healthiest group in the nation. Our clothes and shoes were designed for neatness and comfort. Our needs were provided for. We had little need for money. A taxi to town cost only fifty cents. It was a good opportunity to save.

The CCC had regular days set aside for schooling and a wide variety of courses were offered in health and first aid. There were also courses in both academic and vocational fields. Recreation was provided for leisure hours, and spiritual guidance was a definite part of the camp routine.

I learned in camp that I count; that certain things would be left for someone else to do if I didn't do my part in planning meals, buying food, and so forth. If I neglected any part of my duties, it would hurt my camp buddies. But I also learned that I didn't count any more than anyone else. Even if I was a leader, I didn't dare take more than my share.

I learned that there must be a commanding officer and staff to enforce regulations, and that the easiest way to get along was obedience. I learned that there was ample reward for work well done, and that disobedience to the regulations invariably hurt the entire company.

After six months in Alabama, I graduated from my second food service class. I was prepared for a career in food service when President Roosevelt made his speech in 1941 declaring the entry of the United States into World War II. Even before the speech, many members of the CCC had been drafted or enlisted. Sometimes they came back to visit, always in uniform. World War II was talked about among us, long before America was involved in it. Still, it was hard news. We knew we would be drafted as soon as we turned eighteen.

As it turned out, budgetary and political considerations finally ended the CCC. Our commander announced that the corps would be disbanded, since we were going to war. Too many young men were being drafted for the CCC to continue operating. Those who were not old enough soon would be. The commander himself expected to be in the military shortly.

The CCC was located at various places but we all returned to our military base to be discharged. We were let go in groups so we could take care of the equipment and camp gear that had been issued to us. The CCC provided train or bus tickets for us to return home.

I was seventeen and a half years old. In six months, I would be drafted. Everything I had learned in the CCC had prepared me for life in the military, although I didn't think about it at the time.

We talked about the war at night in the barracks. I was too young and naïve to be frightened. We were looking at glory instead of death, as young men will.

I wondered if I'd ever meet any of my CCC buddies again. As it turned out, I met several on the front line in Italy. It was good to see them again but there was little time to talk. We were fighting Germans at the time.

I no longer recall their names, but the good times we shared in the CCC will always be a good memory, a part of the larger, pleasant and positive experience of my year and a half in the Civilian Conservation Corps. And history has proven it to have been an important part of preparing America to meet the challenge of World War II.

It was a wonderful time in my life as well as the preparation for my future successes, both in the military and in the private sector.

Part Four
Becoming a Soldier

Chapter 9
From CCCs to GI

I had a short visit with my parents. One of my brothers worked in a gun stock factory in St. Louis, Missouri. He urged me to come there and work with him as they were desperately short of help. All able-bodied men were being trained and shipped overseas. Women, symbolized by the hard-working "Rosie the Riveter," were replacing the men in the factories, which were commonly called "war plants" because whatever was produced in them contributed to America's efforts to win the war. Everyone worked as much overtime as possible.

"We need all the help we can get and we need it now," my brother told me.

Before I left, Mama gave me all the money the government had sent to her and Papa while I was in the CCC.

"Papa and I don't need this money," she said. "You earned it. You should have it." She hugged me like she did when I was a little kid.

"Papa and I are so proud of you," she said.

Papa was in his seventies, a little stooped, a little gray, although in good health as far as I knew. "Take good care of yourself," he said.

My parents knew little about the war. They didn't have much access to newspapers or radio. I knew I'd be drafted but had no idea where I'd be going. Neither did they, so it was a worry.

It was difficult to leave them, not knowing when I'd see them again, but I wanted to help the war effort in any way I could before I became a soldier.

I lived in Kinlock Park, St. Louis, with my relatives. My brother drove us to work. When he was off, I took the bus.

The factory, like most factories during World War II, ran twenty-four hours a day. We were lucky to be on day shift. My job wasn't hard. I cut blocks of wood into specific lengths, and then sent them down the line. When they reached the end of the assembly line, they were fashioned into gunstocks.

The saw sliced easily through the hard walnut wood. I cut a lot of those blocks in a shift. Factory work is repetitious but I didn't mind. I could think about anything I wanted to while I did my job. I looked carefully at every piece of wood that passed through my hands. I didn't want any defective gunstocks going to our GIs.

———

We got to play a little, too. There were several clubs in St. Louis and they were packed with young people every night. With the future so uncertain, everyone wanted to enjoy life while they still had the opportunity.

It was in one of the clubs that I first saw and heard Ethel Waters. She was young, just getting her start as a singer. It didn't matter how noisy a club was, when Ethel Waters began singing, everything got quiet.

When that girl sang *Stormy Weather*, it sent chills up and down my spine. She had tremendous natural talent and a great stage presence. I bet every guy in that room thought she was singing just to him. She had a figure, too, big soulful eyes and a winsome smile. It was pretty obvious she was on the way up in show business.

Many years later Ethel became a gospel singer and traveled with the Billy Graham Crusade. She was old and in poor health, but when she sang "His Eye Is on the Sparrow," she still had the gift.

———

Before I knew it, six months had passed and I received the "Greetings" letter telling me I was drafted, just like millions of other young men. Uncle Sam wanted me.

Of course I was scared. I was going into the military and there was a war on.

Becoming A Soldier

The performance of the 92nd Infantry Division sparked many debates, including some about the ethnicity of officers. Some of the military establishment felt that black troops performed better under black officers, but others believed that white officers were better suited to command black soldiers.

Combat experience showed that troops performed best under good officers, regardless of their skin color. For the most part, the American military establishment considered the "experiment" of black combat troops a failure. The black press blamed segregation, while the Army's upper echelons cited racial inferiority, though not all white officers shared that opinion.

A look at the facts, however, suggests that both sides were wrong. The Buffalo Soldiers did indeed break through the Gothic Line. The setback in February 1945 had much to do with the German coastal guns, which survived repeated efforts to silence them.

The 92nd did have its share of problems. In some cases whole platoons were disarmed and arrested because of their performance, although many of the charges against the men were later dropped. It should be noted that, owing to the Army's inability to supply the number of replacements needed by the 92nd, troops who had formerly been absent without leave were sent to the black division from the East Coast processing center. Considering the 92nd's overall success during the Italian campaign, the unit's experience in World War II sounds far more like a success story than anything else.

Black Americans in uniform found themselves in a rather compromising situation during World War II. The black press, almost unanimously opposed to a segregated military, promoted the Double V campaign–a military victory for America overseas and a political victory for the black community at home.

Robert Hodges, Jr. for *World War II Magazine* February 1999.

Chapter 10
Basic Training

On November 22, 1942, I was inducted into the army at Jefferson Barracks, Missouri. I was realizing my dream to become a soldier and I was proud that I would be serving my country. However, I wasn't as naïve as I'd been more than two years earlier, when I'd first seen army uniforms. I listened to the radio and read the newspaper every day. It seemed like the whole world was fighting on one side or the other of a war that Hitler had begun in Europe, and Japan had brought to us at Pearl Harbor. America was fighting on two fronts. Soldiers were wounded and killed every day. Every branch of the military needed more military men. I would soon be one of them.

—

I was shipped to Fort Breckenridge, Kentucky, where I became a member of the Ninety-second Infantry Division, E Company, 370th Regiment, an all-black unit in a segregated military.

As it turned out, of the 900,000 or so black Americans in World War II only one black division saw infantry combat in Europe—the Ninety-second. We had black junior officers; however, most of the higher officers were white, including our Division Commander, Major General Edward M. Almond.

I was assigned to food service because of my CCC schooling and remained there while training to be a combat soldier. I had to go through basic training the same as every other GI .

The training I'd had in the Corps helped me to adapt to military life, but nothing I had experienced before made it any easier. Basic training was very hard and difficult.

We frequently marched five miles before breakfast. The

platoon sergeant decided whether or not we carried a full pack. That set the pace for the day—strenuous, hard training designed to turn us into battle-ready soldiers.

Classroom instructors and field instructors all put the pressure on. We learned to take our rifles apart and put them back together faster than I thought possible. We learned to march in step, to pull the pin on a hand grenade, and then throw the grenade fast and accurately. We were also taught hand-to-hand combat.

At Breckenridge we learned the nuts and bolts of military life and then were taught how to use that knowledge under battlefield conditions. For instance, if our weapon jammed and we couldn't fix it in a split-second, we very likely would be killed.

We were taught the value of fast decisions in hand-to-hand combat, and the consequences of too-slow decisions.

We learned to look out for the man standing next to us. We learned that no matter what befell us, to never let go of our rifles. We learned that every piece of information that was given to us was too important to forget and our lives were dependent on constant vigilance.

After months of being drilled over and over on what we were required to master, we were told we would be sent to Fort Huachuca, Arizona for continued maneuvers.

Before we left Breckenridge, a black general, Benjamin O. Davis, spoke to us.

"You are Buffalo Soldiers," he said. "I am a Buffalo Soldier." He went on to tell us the history connected with the name.

Buffalo Soldiers originated on the frontier as horsemen with the Ninth and Tenth Cavalry, fighting in the Indian Wars and later the Spanish-American War. The heavy buffalo robes the soldiers wore to combat the harsh winters, as well as their black, curly hair and their color, led the Indians to call them Buffalo Soldiers. It was a term of respect, which became a name that stuck to all black GIs.

Buffalo Soldiers served in every war America ever fought since 1866, always in segregated units. Their shoulder patch, with the picture of a black buffalo, was worn with pride, and Buffalo Soldiers always fought with courage.

"Buffalo Soldiers are good soldiers," General Davis said.

"They have made heroic contributions to America—their country. They have distinguished themselves in every war they've ever fought in, with little or no recognition. We are Buffalo Soldiers, " he repeated. "I am proud to be a Buffalo Soldier. You can take pride in being a Buffalo Soldier, also. Wear your buffalo patch with honor and fight your best for freedom and your country."

We all thought it was a hard life at Breckenridge and looked forward with relief to going to Fort Huachuca. We quickly learned we were wrong. We drilled constantly, in nearly unbearable heat. It remained hot and dry the entire time we were there. Arizona has cacti, tarantulas, desert sidewinders and likely some other dangerous wildlife. We shook our shoes out every morning to dislodge anything that might have been sleeping there, and whether marching, drilling or just walking about the camp, we always kept alert so we wouldn't step on anything that might take offense and bite us.

It wasn't too unusual to see some GI walking along, and then suddenly grab his rifle and fire. There would be another dead snake. Some of the guys saved the rattlers, but I never liked seeing them or hearing them.

When we left Fort Huachuca, we knew how to fight a war in a desert. Since Germany and Japan have no deserts, it didn't seem too likely we would have that opportunity, but Uncle Sam wanted us to be combat ready for every possibility.

Our next maneuvers were in the Louisiana backwoods. The weather was really hot—hot and humid. Our uniforms stuck to us like they'd been glued on. We had traded hot and dry for hot and humid. I wasn't too sure it was a good trade.

No more crawling through the desert on our bellies, watching for sidewinders and tarantulas. Louisiana had its own species of dangerous snakes, alligators, biting bugs and flies of all kinds. We were told of a seldom seen black panther that inhabited the dense woods, but thankfully, none of us ever saw or heard one.

We crossed swamps and bayous that sucked us in to our knees. We learned to fall so that our guns didn't get wet or muddy. We learned that when we reached our limit of endurance, we could go one more mile. We learned that we could live with mold, mildew, and hanging moss that clutched and pulled at our clothes.

Because of the difficult terrain and the heat the training got no easier. A lot of guys required medical attention. Infections from insect bites, dehydration, drinking contaminated water, all coupled with intense fatigue, took their toll. We continued training but our hearts weren't in it.

We were relieved to board the troop train to leave Louisiana, even though we were shipping back to Huachuca. Fort Huachuca was starting to look good.

I took one last look from the train window. "The only way I'll ever come back here is if someone makes me," I told the soldier next to me. Fortunately, no one ever did.

Back in Huachuca, we were told we were combat ready but would do review training until it was time to ship out.

One guy wondered why we had to continue if we were already good soldiers. "The Germans are good soldiers, too," the platoon leader told him. "If you want to win this war and stay alive, you have to be better."

Maneuvers continued. We crawled across open terrain and through barbed wire fences, this time with live ammunition shot about a foot and a half above our heads, to see how we'd react under fire. The platoon leader kept yelling instructions reminding us it was live fire and battlefield conditions.

I didn't need anyone to tell me to keep my head down. I inched along on my elbows hoping none of those bullets were fired too low.

Several soldiers panicked and got shot, none seriously. A few got hung up in the barbed wire. All of them were carted off to the hospital. Most of us remained calm under live fire and accomplished our objective, in spite of being afraid. The Buffalo Soldiers were ready for combat.

Chapter 11
Disaster Strikes

We had about a month left at Huachuca. Having completed combat training, I was back in food service. We used four large gas stoves outside the kitchen to heat water for the troops. It was heated in forty-gallon containers, transferred to a truck, and then hauled to the field. Once we got it going, there was no need to watch it.

One day there was a dull boom, followed by a rapid series of sharp explosions. I raced outside. The stoves were on fire! Flames shot straight up and fire billowed out from all of them. The four water containers split. Water and steam erupted into an inferno—all in a matter of seconds. I had to shut off the gas! I ran toward the stoves. A hissing, roaring wall of fire came at me like a runaway freight train. It seemed like the whole world was on fire and I was in the middle of it. There was nothing I could do. I turned to run but I wasn't fast enough. What felt like a hot claw dug into the back of my leg and knocked me to the ground. That was it.

Two days later I woke up in the hospital, pain shooting up my leg. The doctor came in to see me.

"It will be quite a while before your leg heals," he said. "I had to do a skin graft for the burn. That corner piece from the stove that stuck itself in your leg hit with a lot of force. The muscle and nerve damage will take time to return to normal."

"How long before I get out of the hospital?" I asked.

"Don't rush it. We'll keep you in bed a few days to give the graft a chance to take."

My leg was propped up on a pillow. It hurt constantly.

I couldn't imagine it hurting any worse if I did walk on it. Several days later, when I was allowed to walk with stand-by assistance, I found out I was wrong. Still, I was glad to be on my feet. I figured if I could walk, I could ship out.

Some of my buddies came by. They filled me in on the accident. It seems a gas line erupted and caught fire. The intense heat tore the water cans and stoves apart. The gas fed the fire until late evening. It finally died down enough so that the firemen could put it out. In the meantime, firemen and fire trucks stood by to prevent the buildings from burning.

I took a ribbing for my misguided attempt to control the fire.

"You were the only one that went left," one guy said. "All the rest of us went right. What's the matter, Ollen? Didn't your mom and dad teach you which hand to write with? Or are you just left-handed?"

They told me that when they saw me fall and not get up, a couple of GIs ran back, grabbed me by the arms and dragged me out like a sack of potatoes. My pants leg was on fire.

"Man, you're lucky to be alive," a buddy said.

I was. And lucky to have buddies who would risk their own necks to save mine, the kind of buddies any GI would want.

My friends Carl Stokes and Parren Mitchell came by frequently. Parren talked, as always, about his future after the war. He wanted to be an attorney. It would be his stepping-stone to politics, where he would be in a position to help blacks as well as other minorities, whites included.

Carl and I also wanted careers in public service. We just weren't sure what we wanted to do. I had taught Carl to be a mess officer and met Parren through him. Carl leaned toward politics but he liked the military also.

"Might as well like it, " he said. "I'm in here for the duration of this war."

In the military, everyone has a lot of buddies. Everyone speaks the same language and has the same goals. Friends are something else. Parren, Carl, and I were friends. We maintained our friendship throughout our lives, although at times years went by without much contact.

As I felt better and gained more mobility with less pain, I became more and more bored with the hospital routine. I was ready to rejoin my outfit.

I asked the doctor to release me. "I can come in every day for treatment, until we ship out," I said.

"Private Hunt," he said, "You won't be shipping out. I don't believe you understand the severity of your injuries. We are not talking days or even weeks of treatment. We are talking months of treatment. You will not be rejoining your outfit. I have already spoken to your commanding officers about this."

Trying to convince him otherwise was useless. I called both my unit commander and battalion commander and begged them to talk to the doctor on my behalf. Both had visited me in the hospital and said, "If there's anything we can do for you . . ."

I told them I was there to fight for my country and I wanted to go with my unit.

The doctor discharged me with lots of instructions. The medics were to check my leg every day and change dressings. I was to do no more marching than was absolutely essential. There was restriction after restriction.

Finally, the doctor stopped talking about all the things I should do and shouldn't do.

"Private Hunt," he said. "At both your commanders' requests, I am discharging you from the hospital. However, I think I should tell you that as you grow older, you will have problems with your leg."

I didn't know then just how right he was.

Chapter 12
Shipping Out

We boarded a troop ship at Camp Patrick Henry, Virginia—destination, Italy.

German submarines patrolled the Atlantic Ocean. Their job was to sink troop ships. To avoid them and the winter storms, we traveled a longer, but safer route.

Our trip was pretty smooth, but some days we really rocked and rolled. Quite a few soldiers got seasick, but the medics were there to take care of us. There wasn't much they could do except advise us to eat a lot. The medical thinking was that the more we ate, the less likely we'd be sick. I saw quite a few GIs leaning over the rail. Some stayed in their bunks a lot. I felt queasy a few times but never did become sick.

I spent most of my time on deck. I liked the smell of the salt air, watching the sea gulls and the constantly changing pattern of the ocean. We were at sea one or two days when an officer came on deck.

"Sir," one of the enlisted men asked. "How far are we from land?"

"Two miles," the officer said. "Straight down." It was a sobering thought.

After I got to Italy, I heard about a GI who fell overboard from a troop ship that was crossing the Atlantic.

A lot of guys yelled. "Man overboard!" The ship didn't slow down. Someone threw a life preserver. Once—twice—three times the man's head rose above the water. Then he was gone! I heard that one GI ran to an officer and begged him to stop the ship and rescue the soldier.

"We can't endanger the lives of two thousand men attempting to rescue one," the officer told him. "There are German U-Boats just looking for a sitting duck. A man can't last in these waters more than five minutes. It takes a lot longer than that to slow down a ship this size." The GI telling the story said he hadn't been able to get the picture out of his mind.

———

The medics checked my leg, changed my bandages and replaced my brace daily.

Even on ship we had responsibilities. We were required to do general cleanup of our area and attend training classes. The officers occasionally gave speeches on whatever they thought important.

One of the commanders stressed the seriousness of the situation we were heading into.

"Remember," he said, "This is war. All of us are going into combat. Some of us are not coming back." He told us to remember our training and to use it, if we hoped to survive.

We had plenty of free time, too. I wrote a letter home, something I had tried to do monthly ever since joining the CCCs. As always, I left out anything that would worry my parents. I steered clear of card sharks, but enjoyed a friendly game with Carl and Parren.

Our friendship grew as we talked about our involvement in World War II. Always, we went on to speak of our future after the war. All three of us were confident we'd have that future. A lot of other GIs thought the same, but died on the battlefield. We were three of the fortunate ones.

———

On the way to Italy, we stopped at several countries, mostly to take on or unload supplies. I always stayed at the rail to see what was happening, but often that was very little as most of the stops took place at night.

An exception was Africa. As we drew near the coast, I saw long lines of animals moving, all in the same direction. Lions, elephants, zebras, rhinos, and all kinds of animals, thousands and thousands of them, moved along peaceably, as though there was no food chain and as though no animal preyed on another to survive.

We got close enough to see the light, shimmering dust created by the migrating animals. We heard them calling to each other. There was no fighting. Each species had its own agenda.

"Wow! Can you believe that?" I said. "They're all getting along."

"They feed morning and evening," one guy said. He grinned. "They probably just had breakfast. Right now they're one big, happy family."

I could not take my eyes off the moving herds. I have never seen anything so beautiful, before or since.

Cameras were not a common thing back then. I've often wished I had some pictures or a video of that amazing scene, one I will never forget. I watched until I no longer could see them.

Part Five
WWII—Serving In Italy

Chapter 13
Naples

Sixteen days after leaving the United States, we arrived in the harbor at Naples, Italy. It was a busy, hectic scene. Ships were there from other countries with identifying flags. Men in various uniforms and Italians in local garb, some quite colorful, swarmed over the docks. People were everywhere, all of them in a hurry. It looked like an Italian version of New York City.

Naples harbor and the town held so much activity and so many people that it was only later we found out that news of our arrival had brought black soldiers from the Ninety-second Division to greet us.

I don't know how they managed to get leave. Once we found out they would be able to see us leave the ship and head to the front, we decided to put on the best military show we were capable of. Wearing full battle dress with the black buffalo shoulder patch, we moved into unit formation, then marched away, every man in step, weapons in place. The watchers gave us a thunderous cheer.

We were told we'd be heading to the front as soon as we got our outfit together. In the meantime, I was one of the lucky ones who got a pass to go into town a few evenings.

I think Naples is noted for its museums and architecture, but I didn't see much of either. All GIs are the same. We walked the streets and looked at the sights, especially the girls. As far as I know, all Italian girls are pretty and all Italians are friendly.

We'd stop in the local taverns and sample the beer and wine. The Italians made us welcome. We didn't speak Italian but some of them spoke broken English so we carried on conversations with them. The Italians, as a whole, treated us just like they treated the white GIs. There was no racism. As far as they were concerned, we were all equal. In fact, a few of the girls seemed to be flirting with some of my buddies. What a morale booster!

One local fellow told some of us that Hitler and Mussolini had parted company just before we got there. It seems Mussolini lied to Hitler about the number and placement of his planes. Hitler inspected Mussolini's planes in Naples, and then again in Rome. He somehow discovered he had inspected the same planes twice. By then Hitler had conquered so many countries he thought he didn't need Mussolini. Mussolini ended up surrendering to America. Then Italy declared war on Germany, but most Italians had no guns so the partisans did the only fighting. From what I saw the partisans fought bravely against the Germans. They had to—it was their country.

One thing about the Italians, they loved to talk. They could go on and on about nearly anything.

Hitler was a favorite topic. One story was that when he made speeches, which he seemed inclined to do often, he'd scan the crowd for pretty, blond-haired, blue-eyed girls. He would choose one and have his driver pick her up and take her to Hitler's place. After a couple of days, he'd have the driver return her to where she came from.

"Hitler!" the Italians would say. Then they'd finish in Italian so we didn't know what they were saying, but we were sure it wasn't complimentary. Especially when they'd spit after saying his name.

Chapter 14
The Front Lines

Less than two weeks after we reached Naples, we were on the front lines of World War II.

My part of the line was in a grape field near Florence, Italy.

"Dig in!" ordered the sergeant.

He didn't have to tell us twice. German bombs and shells came closer every minute. Being a farm boy, I was no stranger to a spade or shovel, but I got a quick crop of blisters digging in that hard, rocky ground.

The shelling continued without letup, but we remembered our training and held the line. After a few days of constant fighting, the Germans retreated from our artillery. We were rookies, and very pleased to be told we had performed like battle-hardened veterans.

—

The front line changed frequently. When the bombing and heavy artillery stopped, the foot soldiers went into action. Sometimes the Germans advanced. Sometimes we advanced. We were always targets, so we moved cautiously, foot by foot, sometimes tree to tree, and alert for enemy movements. Once the first shot was fired, it quickly became a firefight, which often escalated into hand-to-hand combat.

I felt like I was part of a horror movie. Real life could not be like this, not even on a battlefield. When my mind couldn't deal with the reality and death I was caught up in, I operated on instinct. We all did. Otherwise, we could not have continued and survived.

War takes persons of the highest humanity and intelligence and places them in a position so that they operate on the most primitive thinking—kill or be killed. Placed in such a position, each one does what is necessary to survive.

Even though a soldier may be fighting for the highest good, he cannot carry the memories of warfare with him. They are too terrible to think about, so they migrate to wherever the thoughts we can't deal with go. A man I know refers to it as "a sacred place." I can think of no better words.

I made my peace with my World War II memories long ago. I will let buried memories lie.

———

I have yet to meet a GI who fought in World War II who willingly talks about those painful memories. When I think about what I witnessed in the war, it is not in any particular order. Nobody focuses on a calendar in combat. Soldiers focus on the next battle and pray they will get through it.

My buddies and I fought in places with unfamiliar names, some places that we didn't get the names of, and some places with names that we quickly forgot. Some are still with me after all these years. The Apennines, of course, and the Gothic Line that described Field Marshall Kesserling's line of battle, the Arno River, the Serchio Valley, the Po Valley, Casina, Veraggio, Pietrasanta, and Pisa. If I tried hard, I might recall more, but to think of places where I fought is to bring up memories best left alone.

———

Once we took a position, it was ours only as long as we could hold it. The same was true of the Germans. Some positions we fought for more than once. We paid a heavy price in casualties. Casualty is an official military word for dead or wounded. It doesn't sound as ugly or final, but it means the same.

There are truths a soldier soon finds out regarding the military and war. One is that everybody speaks the same language. This fosters camaraderie. Everyone is a buddy. You look out for that buddy and he looks out for you. Another truth is that death respects no person, rank, color, or ties of friendship.

Once the Germans began shelling or bombing, we hunkered down and waited it out. It didn't matter where we were. When the shelling stopped and it looked safe, we'd go behind the lines for food supplies. It was always C-rations, prepackaged meals that were supposed to be varied. For the most part, beef alternated with chicken. If a GI got the same meal two days in a row, he didn't complain too much. The troops knew we risked our lives to bring them food and water. When it was too risky to leave the foxholes, we all did without.

World War II brought Spam to the public's attention. The GIs were glad to get that, too. There were a lot of jokes about Spam, but it couldn't have been too bad. It's still around.

The Specialist-4's job was to go with us to get supplies. Sometimes we had to go 100 to 150 miles to get them, if it wasn't safe to store them closer. We usually gave each soldier three to four days' rations and hoped they wouldn't run out before we could safely make another trip.

When we neared the front line with supplies, I usually called my commander to find out if it was safe to proceed. Sometimes we had to wait but it was worse for the hungry and thirsty GIs who first had to fight the Germans before they could eat or drink. It's hard to be hungry, but to be thirsty and have no access to water is an ordeal.

At one point, five of us were responsible for getting food to two hundred GIs. And, for sure, we did it with our rifles on our backs, using them when we needed to..

On one return trip, it was much quieter than usual so I figured it was safe to proceed. As we moved along, we saw dead soldiers in some of the foxholes, but most were empty.

We continued, and then saw four or five soldiers on the hill above us. When we got a little closer, we realized they were Germans.

We grabbed our guns and fired a few rounds. One German fell forward. His buddies grabbed him and began pulling him to safety. We ran! Miraculously, they did not shoot at us.

We had been very foolish. The front line had changed while we were away and we had gone behind enemy lines. I never failed to phone the commander again.

While we were behind the lines, our outfit might move forward or fall back to regroup. Sometimes it took a while to find them. It was even harder to find them if we got separated from our unit while fighting at night. Field phones could give away our position and the enemy might gain an advantage.

If we couldn't locate Company E, we attached to the nearest unit we could find until we could get back to our own. Getting separated from a unit sometimes created problems. Until a soldier found his outfit, he was usually listed as missing in action (MIA).

Some such paper definition led to my insurance being cancelled, something I didn't find out until many years later. I had to go to Washington, D.C. to straighten that out.

As one GI said, "I never was missing in action. I was just temporarily misplaced for a few hours."

Chapter 15
Time Out for the Medics

The stateside military doctor who ordered daily treatments and dressing changes for my badly burned leg didn't take into account that the medics in the field would be so busy treating the wounded that they would have no time to follow his orders. I was lucky if they took care of my leg more than once a week.

Consequently, it became infected and I was pulled off the line for treatment. That lasted a month. During that period, I spent quite a bit of time in the city of Florence. I found it more appealing than Naples. Naples is beautiful as well as colorful, but the pace at that time seemed close to frantic.

By contrast, Florence had statues and carvings in concrete, as well as amazing three-dimensional friezes, and a much slower pace. It struck me as an artist's town. I walked along the streets and enjoyed everything I saw.

The people of Florence were pleasant and as accepting of the Negro soldier as the residents of Naples had been. The racism and discrimination so prevalent in the United States was not present in Europe as near as I could tell. It was a great feeling.

I became acquainted with a wonderful Italian family. The father had his own business that I frequented. I soon became a regular dinner guest at their home. Before I returned to the front, the father hinted that if I should marry the oldest daughter, I would be taken into the business as a partner.

They were good people. I liked them very much. The sixteen-year-old daughter was pretty and smart, just a real nice girl. I enjoyed her company. She enjoyed taking walks and talking with me. We had a good friendship, but I had not thought beyond that. In my heart, I knew I was way too young for marriage. Still, I maintained contact with them throughout the war and for a time afterward.

I knew several soldiers of the Ninety-second who married Italian girls. Some settled in Italy after the war, and some returned to the States with their brides.

Over the years, whenever my leg begins to hurt more than usual, I'm reminded of that "time out" from the war. The daily treatments were painful back then, but still I remember it as a peaceful, pleasant interlude in my life when I enjoyed the beautiful city of Florence, and the friendly townspeople.

I recall that wonderful family who welcomed me into their family circle. I am still grateful for their friendship and hope that life has been very good to them.

———

The leg healed slowly, or so it seemed to me. At last the doctor said the infection was gone but the burn itself needed daily treatments and dressing changes.

"You won't get that on the front lines," he said, referring to the treatments. "I'm recommending that you be discharged."

I balked. "I won't leave my outfit," I told him. "I'll go AWOL first. I'm not going home till this war is over."

"On the front lines, the wounded are a priority," he said. "Without daily treatments, you'll be back here with another infection. Next time we might not be able to save your leg."

"Then show me how to do it," I told him. "When the medics can't make it, I'll do the treatment myself."

———

When I got burned in basic training, the doctors wanted to give me a medical discharge. Parren Mitchell encouraged me to leave the service and find a career in the private sector.

"It's a white man's war," he said. "We're fighting for other people's freedom. I don't see anyone offering us that privilege. Freedom is not separate restaurants and separate bathrooms."

When I returned from behind the lines after being treated for infection, carrying my own medical supplies, he couldn't believe it.

"So now you're a fighting soldier, cook, and medic," he said. "They should have discharged you."

"They wanted to," I said. "I told the doctor I'd go AWOL first. I'm staying with my outfit."

Throughout the war, the U.S. military struggled with manpower problems and sometimes the way they handled injured soldiers and soldiers who got separated from their units put the troops in even greater danger. A GI needed to stay with his buddies because they would look out for him in combat and he would look out for them. Soldiers who got separated from their units were sometimes assigned to a redeployment center—"repple-depple" they used to call it—and he could be re-assigned to another unit that might look at a new member as just an outsider, a friendless casualty waiting to happen. That's one of the reasons it was important to stay with your unit. That and the fact that we really cared for each other. Of course, black GIs couldn't be put just anywhere.

Parren understood my loyalty to my buddies, a loyalty he shared. He simply thought I was being unrealistic, and that I should accept the medical decision.

Parren was a unique individual. It seemed like he always knew the path he would take in life. Carl Stokes and I weren't that certain of our future. My life unfolded gradually, one step or decision leading to another, and I have been satisfied with that. Carl liked military life ("If you discount the war," he said), but he was also drawn to the world of politics. He was a natural at both.

Parren's attitude toward the war was shared by most black GIs. "What am I doing here?" was an often-asked question. "All this freedom the politicians talk about sure isn't applied to Negroes."

It is a measure of the many Buffalo Soldiers that, in spite of discrimination, they fought bravely and well.

Parren was a good soldier while he served in the military. There is no doubt he would have risen through the ranks and become a great officer if he had stayed in. But his heart and mind were elsewhere. He achieved what he set out to do. When World War II ended, he found the United States was not so grateful for his contribution to their war efforts.

He was a Negro, a second-class citizen. Refused admission to college because of his color, he went to court and won.

He became the first African American to graduate from the University of Maryland, a school that is a heartbeat away from our nation's capital. He became an attorney, as planned, and entered politics. His goal was to abolish the system that discriminated against women and blacks.

He was senator of the state of Maryland for two terms, where he formed the Minority Business Enterprise Legal Defense and Education Fund. The foundation has done many things for the cause of civil rights and equal opportunity.

Parren has spent his life fighting for the rights of others. He fought well and successfully in the political arena. He also fought well and courageously on the battlefield, risking his life to save a comrade. I've always been proud Parren Mitchell was my friend.

Chapter 16
Sharing a Foxhole – Saving a Life

Foxholes are not Government Issue. They don't hand you a foxhole with your fatigues and mess kit. Every GI has to dig his own. For that purpose, the military issued a small fold-up spade. Next to a rifle and ammunition, it was the most important piece of gear needed to survive.

The foxhole, which cost sweat, blisters, and an aching back, was the only shelter available at the front. A soldier would eventually need to leave that shelter because of an overfull bladder or the urge to defecate. Depending on the situation, we could sometimes run behind a tree, relieve ourselves, and then run back to the safety of our foxhole. However, we were sometimes pinned down in our foxholes for long periods of time, so we dug a hole to one side of our foxhole, used it for elimination, then covered it with soil. That allowed us to answer the call of nature and still save our skins.

Foxholes were temporary accommodations as the fierce fighting shifted one way or another. As we captured new territory, we dug another foxhole. You were at a disadvantage if you were a big guy. I'm over six feet tall so I had to dig a little deeper than the short guys did.

The amount of time it took to dig a foxhole varied according to how soft or hard the ground was, if it was a muddy mess or the wind was blowing loose soil into our eyes, but mostly it depended on how close the Germans were and how much enemy fire we were getting.

Foxholes were never comfortable places to be. In heavy rains we stood in muddy water to our ankles, wet to the skin. In snow, we shivered inside our sleeping bags, unable to stay warm. We longed for a shower and a hot meal. As one GI groused: "At least they could let us fight the Germans long enough to get warm."

When artillery fire was sporadic, it was tempting to get out of the foxhole during the lull. That's the time we needed to worry about snipers. During one such lull, Parren Mitchell took a chance and gambled that no snipers were looking his way. He was a lot closer to my foxhole than his own when all of a sudden the Germans opened up with heavy artillery fire.

"Ollen," he said, "You got room in there?"

"Get in, Parren!" I squeezed to one side as he dropped beside me.

"Wow," he said. "That was really close, Ollen. You saved my life."

If I was going to be pinned down, there was no better company than Parren. Parren never talked about the circumstances we were in because of the war, other than to question a system that put blacks in a segregated unit, where we fought for other people's freedom. He was a real foxhole philosopher.

"When I get out," he said, "I'm going after a law degree. Then I'll be in a position to run for public office. It's the only way minorities will have a voice, with someone qualified fighting for them. I'm going into politics and I'm going to change the system. Freedom and opportunity should be for everyone, not just a select few."

"First, we have to win this war," I said. "Then we can look at a future."

Shells exploded way too close for comfort.

"If we're still here," I added.

"I'm not going to get killed, Ollen," he answered. "I have a whole lot of living to do."

The longer we sat there, the more it sounded like each shell was coming straight at us. That was a peculiar thing about being in a foxhole. We questioned every shell. *Is that one going to hit me? Did I pick the right foxhole? Should I move out?* Every shell sounded like "my" shell.

The artillery sounded like it was on top of us. Bombing was intense. The noise was deafening.

"I'm just a target here. I'm leaving," I said.

"Stay, Ollen. No matter how bad it sounds, this is the safest place we can be right now."

I took his advice. If I hadn't, the ground fire would have cut me to ribbons.

Parren always said I saved his life that day. I've always said he saved mine by talking me into remaining in my foxhole until the shelling was over. We both survived the day.

Sadly, a lot of fine young men did not.

———

There were no better soldiers than the Buffalo Soldiers. We fought, time after time, with all the courage and fortitude, all the energy, and all the faith we had. I never saw or heard of a Buffalo Soldier engaged in fighting in World War II who behaved in a cowardly or unmilitary way. We were committed to fighting and helping to win the war. To the last man, we fought bravely and well.

———

I recall First Lieutenant John Fox, who died after ordering his own men to fire on his position, as he was being overrun by the enemy. Thirty-eight years later, President Clinton awarded Fox the Distinguished Service Cross. First Lieutenant Vernon Baker was another soldier who received the belated acknowledgement from President Clinton. From what I understand, the soldiers of the Ninety-second received more than 12,000 decorations and citations for their bravery and sacrifices in combat. The Ninety-second broke through the fiercely defended Gothic Line, and captured or helped to capture nearly 24,000 prisoners of war. These statistics alone put to rest any debate about our dedication and valor.

———

Early in the war I had put some thoughts on paper encouraging the Negro race to buy savings bonds and stamps. I had planned to publish it in the military newspaper, but never got around to it. I offer it now as an example of my thinking at that time.

BUY DEFENSE STAMPS AND BONDS

It is time for the Negro to begin to think seriously of the postwar days. That is when the smoke of the battles has been cleared away and every race and group will set out to adjust to a new condition that we cannot conceive now. It may be such a thing that every man will be struggling for himself and God for all. It will be a mighty fine thing for every Negro to go to some locked box or closet and pull out savings bonds and stamps and cash them in to tide him over during the period of readjustment.

Most of us are spending too much money on what we call a good time, and other social pleasures. We should realize now that the race doesn't have as many sympathetic friends as it once had. We are living in a time now when every "tub must sit on its own bottom."

The white race knows that Negroes are free. They are getting paid in many instances as other workers. They are rapidly becoming an educated race. It's human nature for people to help those who help themselves.

If you aren't able to pay for a $25 bond, then start buying stamps, which can be purchased as low as ten cents.

Chapter 17
In Action

First and foremost, we were all fighting soldiers. After that, we were assigned whatever the military chose to give us. I was responsible for food supplies. The supply sergeant was responsible for the ammunition. An ironclad military rule was "Never outrun your supply lines." This referred to ammunition and food, in that order of importance.

My unit commander, Captain Counts, once told me I had the most dangerous job in the outfit.

"Ollen, be careful!" he said. "German snipers will shoot you at any opportunity."

I knew he was right but I also felt I had to do the best I could on the job I had been given. It was hard to think of people being killed because they were taking food to hungry men.

Captain Counts was the bravest man I ever met. I once saw him leave the command post and walk toward a nearby building. A German machine gun opened up. Bullets stitched up dust balls from the dirt road moving in a neat row right alongside him. He didn't look down or change his pace. He continued and went into the next building. Not a bullet touched him!

While he ignored danger, although not in a foolhardy way, he did talk about death a lot. Maybe he had a premonition. He was killed on Pietrasanta Hill.

What a sad day. He was liked and respected by all. Captain Counts and I were close. That really hurt. We prayed. We cried. Then we did the only thing we could do. We continued fighting, driving the Germans back relentlessly.

There are other memories I can't forget—like the cries of the wounded, which come with every battle. The medics did a heroic job but they could not be everywhere at once, and did not always reach a soldier in time to save his life. I will always remember one brave boy from Alabama who lay wounded on the battlefield all night. The medics got to him next morning under covering fire from us.

———

The Germans had a gun that, when fired, made several strange sounds. We called it "the screaming meemie." The sound of that shell would almost drive a man crazy. We had a platoon sergeant who was pulled from the line after a series of traumatic events, then exposed to the sound of the screaming meemie for too long. Shell shock can happen to anyone given the right circumstance.

One guy went off the deep end and shot a gold leaf off a major's shoulder. Unbelievably, the uniform wasn't marred and the officer was unhurt. The GI was taken to the stockade from which he quickly escaped. Many years after the war ended, I heard he had married an Italian girl and was still living in Italy, but the military didn't have his address.

———

Minefields were a major hazard. The Germans had placed many mines where they hoped we'd step on them. Once we knew where the minefields were, we strung strips of tape on a line, showing where it was safe to walk. One GI apparently didn't understand that or was dazed because he walked into the minefield. Parren Mitchell got wounded helping him out.

Many years later when he was being considered for a medal, Parren asked me to go to Washington D.C. and make a statement about how he had been wounded, As it turned out, I didn't need to go. President Clinton awarded him his long overdue medal.

Many, many people, including children, have been crippled or killed by mines, long after wars have ended. Mines are put to a terrible use and that use is not restricted to the military.

I appreciate the efforts of people like the late British Princess Diana who call for the elimination of land mines in warfare. Land mines should be abolished.

———

One day a war correspondent showed up. He interviewed two other soldiers, and then began asking me questions. He had hardly begun when the Germans started bombing. "I'll finish this interview later," he said. We never saw or heard from him again.

———

Missing in action (MIA)—that's a term a lot of people simply don't understand. Most people think it refers to someone held prisoner, as many GIs were in the Vietnam War. They think of someone dazed, a victim of shell shock. Or they think of a GI who went AWOL, married a local and disappeared into the culture of a foreign land, because the GI's parents wouldn't accept a wife from another country. I know of parents who, twenty years after World War II ended, expressed a certainty that their son was safe and alive, a victim of amnesia or marooned on a desert island—in fact, anywhere but dead. Many people seem to think that if there is no body, there was no death.

It's simply not true. When ships were sunk, men went down with them and when bombs exploded, men died. The blunt truth is when a bomb hits a man, there is often nothing left to identify. Bombs blow up what they hit. To chat with a buddy before a bombing raid and then have him disappear can shatter the most battle-hardened veteran.

It is worse to find a small remnant of what used to be a human being. It is small wonder that a GI who finds a combat boot with part of a foot in it becomes unable to function. Men became glassy-eyed for days or they screamed and cried for hours. Sometimes they overcome it if they can bury the memory. If not, they generally turn to alcohol or drugs. Either way, when they reach this crisis stage, they can no longer function as a soldier. "Shell shock" is the verdict and they're out of the military.

Army life in World War II was day to day, never knowing what would happen next, or whether we would see tomorrow. And if we did, which of our friends would be gone. There is no use for anyone to try to make any sense out of war. It can't be done.

My buddy Otto Greer somehow ended up behind the

lines. He realized it when he saw two German soldiers coming toward him. He turned and ran. Both the Germans did the same. No one fired a shot. They all lived to fight another day. Another day when I was returning to the line, I ran into two German soldiers who had somehow gotten behind our lines. We traded shots, and then ran. No one got hurt.

One day we were on the line and the S-4 came up to see if we were getting enough food supplies. When he passed us and walked into the open, we heard a "thunk." He crumpled without a word, shot by a German sniper. He was dead before he hit the ground. We cried and we prayed. But the grief never left us and it increased with our many losses.

Our company clerk—he was just a kid—actually got married two weeks before shipping out. He talked about after the war, where they'd live, what he'd do for a living and how they both wanted a family. "I've got a future," he'd say with a big grin. We'd hardly got to the front lines before a sniper's bullet killed him.

I am still thankful that I was spared ordeals that others had to endure. Prayers and tears held most of us together. I was raised with a strong faith in God but more than once it was tested to the maximum.

In early winter, it turned cold. We figured the fighting would slack off, so we decided to give the troops a real Thanksgiving dinner – turkey and all the trimmings. We went behind the lines and set up a field kitchen in a building near the Leaning Tower of Pisa.

Holidays and Sundays don't mean much in wartime, but our company had subsisted on C-rations for so long, we wanted them to have a hot meal.

On Thanksgiving Day, those of us who were responsible for feeding the GIs hand-delivered a hot meal to all two hundred men in our company. It was worth the work and loss of sleep to see them enjoy home-cooked food.

For two nights I slept on a rug in front of the stoves in the building where we had prepared the meal. On the third night we returned to the front lines. That night the Germans bombed the building. I was one day ahead of them. As the guys would say, my number wasn't up yet.

Many times when we delivered C-rations and the fighting was fierce, some of the men were too scared to eat. Some of them ate and then weren't able to keep the food down. At times GIs sat in their foxholes with tears streaming down their faces, but they still did what they had to do.

We once captured a warehouse where a lot of wine was stored. The quartermaster took it behind the lines for future consumption.

Chapter 18
Apennine Mountains to the Po Valley
War Ends

I never attempted to keep track of where I was fighting as the war progressed. Yesterday was forgotten. I concentrated on staying alive and facing the next battle.

In one vicious firefight when we crossed the Serchio River, we cleared the area of snipers and machine guns. According to the military grapevines—often accurate – we captured some enemy positions and some Germans were killed. That was our first major battle, so it is unforgettable.

Then we moved on to our next objective. Week after week, month after month, we fought.

Our greatest test came when we faced the Apennine Mountains, part of the Gothic Line. The natural terrain put the advantage on the side of the Germans—deep, narrow valleys, stark ridge lines, rugged mountains that had no roads and were virtually impassible. There was not even a trail.

The enemy had excellent fortifications on the ridge lines and weapons of all kinds—mortars, machine guns, cannons, antitank guns. They were protected by bunkers built into the mountainside and had barbed-wire barriers. As winter came on with cold, snow and driving rain, it seemed even nature was aiding them. We were without shelter.

On one of our first offensives, Company J was cut to pieces. Lieutenant Mars was killed and more than half the company was killed or wounded.

"Friendly" tanks shelled my company. We had a large number of casualties and halted our advance.

Every company faced incredible resistance from what seemed to be a protected enemy, while we were inviting targets. The Germans had only to wait for us.

General Benjamin O. Davis, Jr. made his own plan. "I want you to melt the mountain," he ordered.

For four days and nights we attacked the enemy without pause. Bombers roared in and out continuously. Every kind of long-range weapon that could be utilized was brought in. The noise was incredible. It was impossible to talk with anyone. It was like trying to sleep in a room full of running jackhammers. We did not care. It was worth it.

When it was over, Germans surrendered by the convoys, marching out with their hands on top of their heads. Sometimes they talked to us. One German looked at me and spoke.

"What did he say?" I asked a nearby Italian.

"He says he's had enough," he translated. "And he wants to know if you'll sell him some cigarettes."

It wasn't over, but it did get easier. There were still Germans on the line and the only way to get them was to go after them.

The extremely steep mountainside was difficult—nearly impossible—to climb. Each of us was a walking target, expecting a bullet any minute. It is a terrible feeling. While some Germans retreated, others waited it out.

Once we got some troops on the mountain, we had the task of keeping them supplied. The only transportation was horses and mules. Horses were flown in from Colorado. The Italians were very generous in giving us the use of their horses and mules. The horses sometimes lost their footing and fell. If they didn't die from the fall, they had to be shot. The Germans sometimes shot the horses to cut off our supply lines. We tried to keep the horses between the Germans and us. We walked as close to the horse's head as possible. If the horse was shot or stumbled, we let go of the lead rope and dived for the nearest cover, which was scant. Not a lot of man-hiding bushes up there.

In spite of the danger, the Italians sometimes led their horses up the steep mountainsides. God bless those brave Italians who helped us all through the war. And thank God for their sure-footed mules. They turned out to be the best way of moving supplies.

The bitter fighting continued on all fronts. Sometimes I felt like I had been fighting forever and there was no end to it.

Bone weary, overcome with fatigue, I still did what I had to do. We all did.

We eventually took the mountains. The Germans were a formidable fighting force but they were cut off from their supply lines.

They wanted cigarettes and offered one hundred dollars for a carton. That was the start of a black market business between American GIs and German GIs. A small can of coffee brought twenty-five dollars.

One Italian traded a few cigarettes to a captured German in exchange for a book.

"Could you read it?" I asked.

"Sure. Enough. It was a book on military cooking. A manual, you call it. No good. I give it away."

"No good? Why not?"

"First page says— 'First capture a field kitchen'."

I shook my head in disbelief. "From the looks of them, they couldn't have captured many," I said. "They all look half starved."

I wish I had that book.

———

Even war has some pleasant memories and light moments. In one small town, we were clearing out an unused building to accommodate an American command post. In the process we carried out boxes of papers and put them alongside the building. The wind blew some of the papers around and a few Italian women picked them up.

We soon found ourselves besieged by angry middle-aged Italian women, who scolded us and took all the boxes away.

What had we done? An older Italian man informed us that we had trashed pictures of Rudolph Valentino. We'd never heard of him, but of course he was the famous dancer and matinee idol of the silent movie era, some kind of a heartthrob.

Overall, the Italians helped us in any way they could. Like most of Europe, their country and their lives were scarred by war. They had next to nothing and were often hungry.

The U.S. Army is the best fed in the world—then and now. When things were quiet, Italian men came to our unit and helped out as best they could by watching the cook pots, washing dishes, and preparing food. They ate with the GIs. When fighting began, we moved them away from direct combat.

We often had to move civilians back for their own safety. It was hard for them to leave their homes, even though they understood the necessity of it. We sometimes used their homes, but we treated them with respect.

———

There was so much sadness, pain, and fear that foxhole talk usually turned into pleasant banter. One day when it was a little quiet, I listened to a couple of nearby GIs. The subject was food—not surprising—home cooking.

One GI said, "When I get home, I'm going to ask my mom to cook me a big, juicy T-bone with all the trimmings."

"Not me," said his buddy. "I'll have to go to a restaurant to get a good meal. My mom burns everything she cooks."

Everyone smiled. It's cornball, but it took our thoughts away from the war, which everyone knew would soon erupt again.

The other main topic of conversation—not surprising either—was women, sweethearts, girlfriends, wives, those that had them and those that didn't. The silent men were the ones that got "Dear John" letters—a different kind of casualty of the war.

———

In Po Valley, I fought alongside Brazilians, Japanese-Americans, Australians and British soldiers. Someone called us a "Rainbow Division."

The British were "by the book" soldiers and sticklers for tradition. They had little food but they had their tea at its proper time, regardless of circumstances.

"Time for a spot of tea?" I'd tease, in my best British accent.

Every Englishman I met was a gentleman and all of them were friendly. Some gave me their addresses and invited me to visit after the war.

A staple to each proper British soldier was Scotch whiskey. They each had their drink—proper amount, proper time—every day. We'd fix them up with food, courtesy of Uncle Sam.

In a welcome lull from combat, I was chatting with an Australian about his homeland.

"Now that you've seen Europe at its worst," he said, "you

ought to see Australia at its best. You'd be mighty welcome to visit, mate."

"I might take you up on that," I grinned. "Maybe I could take a tour riding in one of those kangaroo pouches."

A few of us were laughing and joshing. I noticed a nearby British officer put down his coffee cup and rise to his feet. GIs were scrambling to their feet, watching and listening. What was up? The news traveled faster than an avalanche.

"The war is over! Germany surrendered."

What an eruption of hugs, cheers and tears. We had longed for this day. Most of us never expected to see it. Some of us never did.

A prim and proper British officer engulfed me in his arms. What a bear hug!

"Thank you, Yank," he said. "We would not have made it without you."

May 8, 1945. V.E. Day. Victory in Europe for the allies.

We would be going home soon. We had survived the war after all. It was a bittersweet moment, tears of joy for our deliverance and the deliverance of the European people, and tears of sorrow for those we'd never see again.

Mostly, we wandered aimlessly, talking to our comrades, hardly able to believe it was true. After fighting for so long, we didn't know how to react to the end of our long ordeal.

The one priority we all had was to notify our families that we had survived the war and would soon be coming home.

Part Six
Postwar Military Career

Chapter 19
Postwar Italy and Home

When the war ended, the army began the massive task of shipping troops home. Everyone couldn't go at once. Those of us who had to wait awhile found plenty of things to interest us.

While learning about the Italian way of life, we relaxed. That was much appreciated after months of continuous combat and stress. It is a real hard jolt to go from the horrors of war straight to your normal family life without an adjustment period. Just by luck, I was in one of the last batches of soldiers to be returned home. As anxious as I was to see my family, I've always been glad I had that transition period in Italy, about forty-five days.

We set up kitchens and once more knew what it was to have regular meals. Again the Italians joined us and did little chores to help out. We all ate together. I enjoyed getting to know them.

And showers! We showered every day. What a luxury. No more spit baths with water in a helmet. No more being sent behind the lines every few weeks for a hot bath and clean clothes. I still don't take a shower for granted. I know there are many people in the world who don't have access to one.

There was much talk about occupational forces. The Italians were all for it. They needed help to rebuild their country and they knew it would pump money into their economy, which they desperately needed.

I began to think more and more about making the army a career. I had seen what the military could do in war. I had been part of it.

In the meantime, there was a minimum of duties to perform. Italy was a beautiful place, and the Italians were friendly. We enjoyed ourselves to the fullest.

I spent two weeks in Rome, where I slept in Mussolini's castle and found it quite comfortable. The castle itself was interesting, as was Vatican City, where all the buildings were trimmed with gold and silver. While I had never heard of Michelangelo back in Tennessee, I have not seen anything before or since that compares to his paintings. All over Italy we had the pleasure of observing some of the most beautiful paintings in the world.

In Rome, I met lots of Americans who lived and had businesses there. They were all nice people and very friendly. Rome was probably the most interesting place I visited. While there, a black lady invited a group of us to meet her employees in her medical building. The next day she treated us to lunch at a local restaurant.

An Italian lady fixed us some pizzas and used chicken guts to make the sauce. We gave her some food items as a thank you. As I recall, we all ate the pizzas. They would likely have tasted better if we hadn't known what the sauce contained.

Some of us visited Venice, also. Even after the war and the devastation it left, the beauty of all the places I visited made a lasting impression on me.

We picnicked two and three days at a time, enjoying some of the wine we had acquired during our early days of fighting the war. I had the privilege of seeing grapes stomped for wine. What a festive atmosphere that was.

The war was a terrible ordeal for everyone, but the time I spent with the Italians was always positive and pleasant—before and after the war. They talked about the future and rebuilding their country, with the same positive attitude.

I could not help but think of a Bible verse from Ecclesiastes Mama used to quote, about a time for tearing down and a time for building back. My Mama would have had the same "can do" attitude as the Italians. They are great people.

While I very much enjoyed my postwar stay in Italy, I looked forward to returning to the United States. I shipped back to Fort Patrick, Virginia along with other GIs who had shipped out from there. We were then all shipped to our nearest home location. I went to Jefferson Barracks, Missouri, where I was given ninety days' leave. I lost no time in getting back to my family.

It was wonderful to be back with my parents, relatives, and friends. My family lived in several different places—St. Louis, Chicago, Detroit, and Tennessee. I visited all of them and had a great time. It gave me an opportunity to consider my future. All my relatives were doing well and enjoying life, but as I considered their various careers and lifestyles, I knew I wanted something different.

My thoughts turned more and more toward a future in the occupational forces, a chance to serve others.

I never told my parents about my life on the front lines. Mama would have insisted I get out of the military. So what if the war was over? Mama knew there would always be another war.

It was hard to tell my family I wanted a future elsewhere, but I did.

"Well, Ollen," Mama said, "You always were anxious to get out on your own and accomplish big things. You do what you feel you're called to do. Papa and I are both proud of you. We know you'll come home when you can. And don't worry about us. You've got enough brothers and sisters here to give us a hand if we need one." I was so happy I made that trip.

In 1954, Papa died. Someone called to tell me. After I hung up, I didn't know whom I had talked to or what they had said, other than –"He's gone, Ollen."

I felt numb, like I wasn't in a real world. Other people took over and I did whatever I was instructed to do.

Someone told me to get my things together; the Red Cross was making arrangements to get me home as quickly as possible. I packed my bag, signed all the necessary paperwork, and waited.

At first I didn't grasp what the Red Cross representative was saying. It didn't make sense.

"What?" I asked.

"We find that you have enough brothers and sisters to take care of the arrangements for your father's burial," he repeated. "It is not necessary for you to go home at this time." He handed me the phone. "Your family is on the line. They're waiting to speak with you."

Various family members talked to me. I answered the same questions, over and over. No, I would not be home for the funeral. I could not get a commercial flight in time. The Red Cross had said I didn't need to be there. My father had enough children to take care of whatever needed to be done.

It was true that my father had several children. What the Red Cross didn't seem to understand or care about was that I had only one father and they were depriving me of the chance to say good-bye to him. The family kept in touch. It helped to know what was taking place.

Papa was born in a time when birth certificates were pretty much unheard of. Not even Mama was certain how old he was. Someone dug through some old records and found Papa was born in Virginia in 1865, making him about eighty-nine years old when he died. He was liked and well respected by all who knew him, a successful farmer who owed money to no one. He and Mama raised a large family, all of them well thought of. Papa lived up to the responsibilities of church, community, and family his entire life. It was a long, full life. I took comfort in that.

Chapter 20
France and England – The Occupation

When my leave was over, I reported to Camp Kilmer, New Jersey. From there I shipped to Paris, France, where the United States had already begun setting up the occupation for Germany and other European countries.

There were no warehouses in Germany, so the occupational forces set up a system to send trucks from France and ships from England with food and other supplies to Germany. It was a difficult task because we were short of soldiers. Many of them left the service after the war.

I spent a year in France. When I arrived there, Paris was not the "Gay Paree" I'd heard of. The German occupation had been brutal. Everything looked shabby. The people suffered; they lacked just about everything. Still, their spirits had not been crushed and they were overjoyed to have Americans there. Once again they had freedom.

Several movie stars had homes on the outskirts of Paris and there was a standing invitation to all GIs to attend parties—and there were parties every night. Transportation was provided. I was young. I worked hard every day and partied every night. As elsewhere in Europe, color was no barrier.

Uncle Sam, it seemed, always had plenty of supplies for us. Next to Uncle Sam, movie stars seemed to have unlimited access to the finer things of life. Every day was like Christmas. We were told over and over again how much we were appreciated. We were given all the good times and good things the stars and locals could give us. And being GIs, we were generous to the French.

I found Paris had many interesting people. I met one black man who was originally from Mississippi. He had lived in Paris ever since World War I. I asked him if he ever thought about going back to America. He seemed to think about that for a few seconds.

"I thought about it," he said. "I just never got around to it."

He invited a group of us to his home. We met his wife, a beautiful blonde, who was dressed in a floor-length gown that was very elegant. Their home was what I'd call a mansion. They entertained us as though we were royalty.

I discovered you could meet people from all over the world in Paris, and people from all walks of life. I could speak just enough French to get along.

We appreciated all the celebrations for the United States soldiers, but we never failed to express our gratitude to the brave French men and women who were our allies and who had fought for freedom, just as we had.

While in Paris, I visited museums and other places of interest. Even Hitler's troops could not destroy or steal everything.

The military has lots of rules and regulations. Each one serves a purpose. Convoys are a good example of that. We used convoys to ship food and other necessities to Germany. A convoy is a number of vehicles, few or many, all alike, all loaded about the same, all going to the same destination. A platoon sergeant is in charge of the convoy. He drives a jeep and leads the convoy, setting the speed.

They generally drive twenty to twenty-five miles an hour, twenty feet apart to a predetermined rendezvous point. At that point, the supplies are usually off-loaded to waiting vehicles to continue to the final destination. The empty trucks then return home. On rare occasions, the convoys may trade trucks.

I always enjoyed watching the convoys go by, each vehicle in its proper place, just like a row of marching soldiers.

Nothing is left to chance. Breaks are designated, miles covered in a day are expected to be exact and the convoy is to reach a certain place at a certain time.

It was a very efficient method of moving supplies in postwar Europe. As a bonus, it prevented black market deals on coveted supplies. One of my duties was to check the paperwork when the convoys returned to make sure everyone and everything was in its proper place.

During and following the war, the black market did a flourishing business. A GI might be able to buy a can of coffee for two or three dollars and then sell it for twenty-five dollars. A lot of GIs—white and black—saw a chance to improve their financial future, too. I heard of two of them that had military trucks loaded with gasoline when the war ended. They quickly repainted the trucks and drove off with them. They sold both trucks fully loaded. I'm fairly sure they got caught eventually, but have no idea if the trucks were recovered.

When it comes to something Uncle Sam gives to the military or sells to them cheap and they have the opportunity to sell it at a profit, the thinking often was— "I have it, he needs it, and I can use the money. What's the harm?"

At war's end I was in possession of a truck loaded with cartons of cigarettes. As far as the military was concerned, I was to distribute them to the troops. I would never have been questioned. I could have sold all of them, pocketed the money and no one would have been the wiser. I did what was right. I turned the truckload of cigarettes back in. One of the officers chewed me out for it.

"That was a stupid thing to do, Ollen," he said. "You should have sold them."

Mama would have said, "We taught you right, Ollen." I never had any qualms about sharing with our allies. But when something passed from my hand to theirs, it was a gift that I had paid for.

After a year in Paris, the military sent me to England for nine months, to help with the operations there. The British already had a system in place so did not require a lot of assistance or changes. I instituted a few things to help expedite the shipping of supplies.

While there, I attempted to find the British soldiers I had gotten acquainted with in the Po Valley. I could not find their addresses so I was unsuccessful. The people I met in England were outspoken in their gratitude to America for our intervention in World War II.

"We had nothing left to fight with," one gentleman said with tears in his eyes. "God bless you Yanks."

The British were in desperate straits for long years after the war, but they were stoic about it. A stiff upper lip, they called it; just keep doing the best you can. I found myself wishing we could do more for the British people.

As in all the other countries I visited, I experienced as much of the local culture as I could. England is a country of traditions and the people are proud of that. Their cathedrals rival any found elsewhere in Europe. The "changing of the guard" at Buckingham Palace is a sight to behold. The castles were magnificent. Even in England I was accepted as a person, not as a black person or a Negro.

I sampled traditional British food while there—steak and kidney pie, scones, and a lot of food I don't remember the names of. Something I ate was called spotted dick, a dessert, a most unusual name for something edible, but the British tend to use names for things that I don't understand. I suppose it goes back to some tradition. While in the Po Valley, the British frequently told me I wouldn't know how good tea was until I tasted real British tea. I had some. It tasted just like what I got at the PX.

I was sorry to leave England, but we were short of personnel in France.

———

Back in France, it didn't take long to determine the occupation was working well.

I was sitting at my desk one day and one of the clerks came in. "Ollen," he said, "I have a message for you."

It was from the Italian family who had treated me so well, telling me they missed me and reminding me I had promised to visit them on my return to Europe. When did I plan to return to Italy? I wondered how they had located me and was somewhat embarrassed that once I returned to Europe I'd been either too busy or having too much fun, I had hardly thought of them.

"Tell them I'll be there for a visit when I get time," I said.

I meant what I said at the time, but a few days later, some GIs I knew came by.

"We've put in for Germany," one said. "Everyone that's assigned there likes it. Why don't you come with us?"

Seeing a new place appealed to me. I requested a transfer and was soon on my way to Germany. I never gave a thought to the promise I had made. I was a young GI and wanted to enjoy life. It didn't occur to me to even send them a message.

In later years, I felt bad that I had not gone back to Italy for a visit, as I had said I would. I guess no one ages without regrets.

Chapter 21
Occupied Germany

In Germany, I was assigned to a place named Regensburg as quartermaster of the gas supply company that supplied gas to all military units in the area. Later I was assigned mess steward of the company and transferred to Munich.

There was much work to be done in Munich. After a few months we moved to a large hotel-type building where people were setting up the organization for the occupation.

My company commander and his family. They preferred my mess to the officers' mess, as did many other officers. Circa 1954

An occupational general and his family enjoying eating at my family style mess. Christmas day - 1955

I came up with an idea that no one else had tried, to the best of my knowledge, a method that would allow us to feed large groups of people quickly. I talked to the supply sergeant about ordering equipment for family-style feeding. It was ordered. We sent trucks to pick up some of the equipment in Paris, then to Bremen harbor in Germany to pick up the rest. I found some qualified Germans to install it.

When everything was installed and working well, we were ready to serve. I employed German women as waitresses, the soldiers had a table assignment by section, and a blessing was said at each meal.

In 1948 or '49 Colonel Marcus Ray came to visit as a representative of President Truman. He was quite impressed with the way I ran my mess. As he said, it was new and innovative and it worked very well.

About two years later the occupation was running smoothly. Our company was disbanded and our group had to move on post. Some were sent to school and some were assigned to teach school where needed. I took a teachers' refresher course at Frankfurt and then I was assigned a teaching position.

I received a call from a colonel in Munich asking me if I'd like to return there.

I said, "Yes, sir!" I liked Munich.

He told me what to do to get assigned back to the Fifty-ninth Trucking Company as mess steward.

I again set up family-style meals, which everyone liked. I remained there for several years until the company got orders to move to Nuremberg. When we arrived there, no one was happy. We were all adjusted to Munich. But in the military, you have to follow orders.

The atmosphere in Nuremberg was not positive. As in other towns in Germany, the war had left a deep impact on daily life. The Nuremberg Trials were underway at the time and, mixed with the grief of war and the world spotlight focused on the town, tensions were running high in Nuremberg. It was a painful time for all involved.

———

I was in charge of an integrated company in Germany. We had a mixed platoon of sergeants and squad leaders. One white soldier from Alabama was assigned to our unit. His squad leader was black. He talked to his white platoon sergeant about it. The platoon sergeant sent him to me.

"What is the problem?" I asked the young GI

"My daddy told me when I joined the army, I'd never have to take orders from a Negro," he said.

I certainly did not want to turn a young man against his father. At the same time, I could not let him continue with the racist view he'd been given. The integration of the armed forces had signaled a new era and people had to let go of the old ways of looking at how we were going to live and work together.

Thanksgiving dinner at my mess in Warner-Kaserne, Munich, Germany.

Some of the German civilian staff employed at the Henry Kaserne. A Sharp looking crew. Circa 1954

"Son," I said, "your daddy was wrong."

We talked a long time. I could give him no better advice than what my Mama and Papa had given me many times: treat everyone with respect no matter where they are from, what color they are, or whether they are rich or poor. I told him their guidelines had helped me through life and I wanted him to try them.

"In the military, each person is given the position he is capable of doing. Color has nothing to do with it," I told him. "We are here to serve our country and you will have to take orders from whomever you are assigned to.

"Dismissed."

About three months later, this same soldier requested to talk to me. The platoon sergeant brought him in. It seems he'd had a change of heart. He told me that everyone had treated him well, that he thought I was a nice person, and everything was fine.

"When I get back to the States," he said, "I'm not going home because my daddy taught me wrong. While here in Germany, we have worked together, taken leave together, and are having a good time, black and white."

I assured him that I didn't want to create a problem for him with his family.

"You didn't," he said. "I'm not mad at my daddy. I just can't live where the races are separated like that."

I guess that's how change happens sometimes. One person at a time.

After he rotated back to the States, I got a Christmas card each year for many years, but never one from Alabama. He wrote the same thing each year. "You are a wonderful person. Stay in touch."

After I was discharged and moved to Alaska, I had one card forwarded from Ft. Lewis, but then I lost touch with him.

I ran a consolidated mess in Nuremberg, feeding about five thousand troops three times a day. We had plenty of help. I employed eighty civilian workers plus the GI cooks and mess stewards from all over the company. I had fifteen people whose sole job was to deliver our food. We did a good job. We liked what we were doing and we enjoyed working together. Being in the military in peacetime was a wonderful experience. Military life grows on a person. It gets in the blood, you might say.

I never had a problem in satisfying those I worked under. First of all, I had to satisfy myself that I was doing my job right in the best possible way. I loved what I was doing and appreciated the leeway I was given to change and improve things as I saw fit.

As I walked from the mess with a group of friends one afternoon, several soldiers passed us going the other way.

"Ollen! Ollen Hunt?"

One of them turned, grabbed me and hugged me hard.

Carl Stokes! I hadn't seen him since D-Day. I never knew if he had taken Parren Mitchell's advice. Like me, he was still in the military, but promoted to an officer. I didn't know Stokes was in Nuremberg.

Consolidated mess at Nuremberg, Germany. Ready to serve. Circa 1949

Consolidated mess at Nuremberg, Germany. When we fed the entire post three meals a day, we had several serving lines. Circa 1949

"Come on over to my office," I said. "We have a lot of catching up to do."

First we bragged about how great the Buffalo Soldiers were. "I'll tell you the God's truth, Carl," I said. "Our boys were real soldiers, as good or better than the whites. There were no finer."

"That's so," Carl agreed. "Great fighting men—but oh, God, the losses."

We both choked up as we remembered friends and buddies who had lost their lives in the name of freedom.

We agreed the military was changing. The new recruits had little self-discipline and made it clear they had joined, not from a desire to be of service, but for what they could get out of it. "I'm only here for four years so the government will pay for my education," was a common expression.

Military discipline seemed more lax. Infractions of the rules were dealt with in a more lenient manner.

"When we had a guardhouse and a belt and they were used judiciously, everyone obeyed the rules," I said.

Carl grinned. "I wouldn't say that just anywhere, Ollen."

We couldn't talk about old times without bringing Parren into the conversation.

"Parren is the most intelligent man I ever met," Carl said. "He is brilliant. And he's using his brains to do all the good he can."

"Yeah," I agreed. "And he's got a lot of courage, too—suing a college for admission rights."

"He won, and rightfully so. I have no doubt he'll do everything he plans to do."

Carl mentioned that he was giving serious thought to leaving the service.

"You know, I have family in politics," he said. "Black people and minorities are sick of slick politics as usual. We need to get in the political arena and do something about it. Parren is right."

We met a time or two after that before Carl rotated back to the States.

He graduated from Cleveland Marshal School of Law in 1956 and went into politics, starting as a Democratic member of the Ohio general assembly. In 1967, he had the distinction of becoming the first African American mayor of a major American City (Cleveland), a position he held for two terms. He was general counsel for the United Auto Workers and then served as a municipal court judge for two terms as well. Finally, in 1994 he became U.S. ambassador to the Seychelles.

He got a later start than Parren, but he sure accomplished a lot. While our lives were different and we had little contact, I was always glad Carl was my friend. When he died in 1996 the United States lost a truly good man.

—

While at the SS Kaserne, I set up the same style of family meal service that had worked so well elsewhere. We had a monthly post conference held in the theatre. Awards were given to the best operation company of the month; best mess hall, best motor pool, and so forth. The award decision was made based on inspections. For eight months straight I received the plaque for best mess. The commander once remarked I should come prepared to accept the plaque. I was proud to win the award

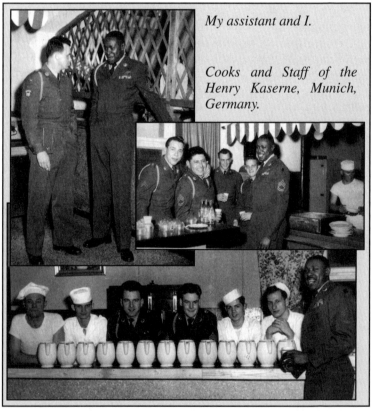

My assistant and I.

Cooks and Staff of the Henry Kaserne, Munich, Germany.

Chapter 22
The Munich Years

In Germany I did many jobs—mess steward, instructor in Cooks and Baker School, first sergeant in the education section, General Inspection Team member, employment officer, and mess steward feeding the entire post at the SS Kaserne. I served all over Germany. The Germans were pleased to have us there.

(left) Two soldiers waiting to be interviewed for jobs in the new type of operation in Henry Kaserne.

(lower left) An officer viewing the menu for Christmas dinner in the mess, Circa 1955

(lower right) Accepting the award for best mess in Granffenwohr, Germany, an award I won for eight consecutive months while stationed at Henry Kaserne. Circa 1956

I was happy when I transferred back to Munich. I loved living in Munich. It was a great town and I liked the people and my job. It was an ideal situation. While there, I was in charge of many picnics and special-occasion get-togethers for the military—often the German people participated.

My years in Munich were some of the happiest years of my life. I am a very social person, always have been. I like people. I think I can truthfully say I have made friends every place I've ever been for any length of time. Germany was no exception.

After World War II, able-bodied German males were scarce. Many of them had been killed; thousands more were incapacitated. Women were raising the kids and doing the farm work. It is my observation that German women are among the most industrious and hardest working of any people I have met. After all, they had to rebuild the country without the help of those who had been killed by the war. Many women turned their homes into guesthouses on the weekend to earn much-needed money. As you can imagine, Germany was very short on the basic necessities of life, such as food and shelter. It was difficult to raise enough food to feed a family and have some left to sell.

As I was single for most of my stay in Germany, I usually drove out into the country, visited small towns and got to know the locals. I enjoyed these excursions very much.

One small town I visited often as I found it pleasant and restful. When I walked into the neighborhood bar, the owner would take his pipe out of his mouth long enough to say "Give Ollen a beer." When I left, he'd say, "Ollen, come back next week."

I met a couple outside Nuremberg—he was German and she was English and we became friends. She once mentioned that the one thing she missed most was tea. The next time I visited, I took a couple of boxes of tea from the BX. I figured while he and I drank beer and talked, she could enjoy her favorite drink.

"Ollen," she said. "Kiss me! You're my hero!" Those British really like their tea!

I was in Germany eleven years and five months. During that entire time, black marketers were a problem. We solved most of it by changing the military scrip once a month. That prevented people from counterfeiting. The GIs, of course, could buy what they wanted. It was pretty hard to prove they sold something instead of using it themselves or giving it away.

When payday came, the GIs would buy at the base exchange and take things to their girlfriends. That was never a problem. Nobody objected to their paying the taxi driver with a pack of cigarettes.

There were those who abused the system and the postwar military faced a huge problem because of them. The people in the black market, as a general rule, got greedier and greedier. It

Birthday celebration for all whose birth date was on that day.

wasn't difficult to figure out that a GI probably didn't need several dozen pair of silk stockings or many cases of coffee. I heard of one GI who somehow managed to acquire and sell something like twenty-seven thousand dollars' worth of goods. He made the mistake of telling someone that, thanks to the government, he had a nice little nest egg and a good future. He rotated back to the States. When he got off the plane, a couple of IRS guys were waiting for him and he ended up doing hard time.

In Europe, after the war, drugs were available everywhere. With everything else scarce and no money to buy with, I never understood how the drug dealers did such a good business. The best I could figure out was that the future looked so bleak to some of those young people, they didn't care any more. That's a sorry state to be in. Nearly all the GIs were approached, as I was.

"Don't you ever come this way and talk to me about drugs," I said.

A snapshot of me leading the parade in Soldier's Field, Nuremberg. Circa 1950s

I became friends with a German man named Hans who owned a castle-like home. It looked like something from the Middle Ages. He rented rooms there to make money and I enjoyed many weekends there. He held a room especially for me so if I showed up it was mine on Friday, Saturday, and Sunday nights.

"If Ollen doesn't sleep here, nobody sleeps here," he'd say.

He was partial to the military. If a GI needed some money before payday, Hans would stake them to four hundred marks.

It was a wonderful place to picnic. Many companies had get-togethers there. I showed Hans how to prepare American food. It was a thrill to catch fish from his small pond and cook them on the spot.

Family Style

Munich, Germany, -- "Bless this food we are about to receive..." is the familiar blessing heard before each meal served in the Able Co., 2d Inf., mess hall. SFC Ollen Hunt, the mess steward, not only believes this is appropriate, but he feels that his mess hall is run in a manner that can be considered unique in this modern Army.

Sgt. Hunt has renovated the old Pre-War II type of platter service into an up-to-date method of "family-style" service, which many people feel is a great deal better than the "chow-line' method.

Able Co's, mess hall eliminates many of the problems that arise in the ordinary dining room and every member of the company, including the CO, 1st Lt. George E. Roberts, is in favor of the family style service.

Regular meal blessing before eating.

To begin with, this method of feeding the troops does away with some of the familiar complaints that you hear every now and then, in most mess halls. There are no long lines to wait in for each meal, as the entire company sits down to eat simultaneously.

The food is usually more highly seasoned, and better tasting, because Sgt. Hunt and his staff take a little extra effort in preparing the food.

In addition to all this, there is little waste as the member of the company eat only what they want, and how much thy want, rather than the "take everything served method."

One particular feature of the mess hall that allows everything to be done in an orderly fashion is the "rolling service wagon."

He was a great guy, a bachelor, and in spite of the people he was often surrounded with, I sensed he was lonely. He once confided that his biggest regret was not having a child to inherit his property.

I'm in my office at Henry Kaserne, Munich, Germany. Circa 1952-1957

Signing in on Separate Rations in mess hall at Henry Kaserne.

The mess at Henry Kaserne. The GIs enjoyed family style dinning. Saying the blessing before eating in the Henry Kaserne. Circa 1952

After I married, my wife, Hannelore, and our newborn son, Erich, went for a visit. Hans was captivated by our son.

"Oh, if he was mine," he'd say. "If only he was mine."

His one topic was his lack of a son and heir and the emptiness of his life because of it. Finally, he blurted out what was on his mind and in his heart.

"Ollen," he said, "I love this boy. I could give him everything, the family name, the estate, a fine education, anything he wanted. He would be my sole heir. If Erich were my son, I'd have something to look forward to every day. I'd have a reason to build up my estate. To live for oneself only is not good. Please, Ollen, let me adopt Erich. You and Hannelore are still young. You can have a family."

I can only imagine what it must have been like for him to plead with me to give up my son. It was out of the question, of course. I loved Erich as only a new father could. I would have chewed my arm off before giving up my child.

During my tour of duty in Germany, I had only rare visits back to the United States. On a short furlough, I visited various European countries and enjoyed each. All those little countries are connected, but every one is unique, with its own customs, culture, and charm.

I returned to the States in 1951. Someone had put me on orders for Korea. I went to Washington, D.C. and made the right connection to get those orders changed. While there, I also straightened out my insurance mix-up of World War II.

The military sent me to Aberdeen Proving Grounds briefly to inspect poultry for the military before they assigned me back to Germany to the Fifth Paratroopers Division in Munich. I was satisfied with that.

I met Parren in a club in Baltimore, Maryland. He talked enthusiastically of his goals and the progress he was making. Parren had an infectious enthusiasm. In other words, he fired people up.

Over the years, I kept in touch with Parren. I was not to see him again until many years later when I was a businessman in Anchorage, Alaska. Parren's purpose in traveling to Anchorage was to investigate complaints of racism by the Small Business Administration. He stayed at the Captain Cook Hotel and was given the key to the city. He made a speech while in Anchorage talking about his foundation, one that furthered education for minorities.

While in the States, I visited two of my sisters and a nephew in Maryland, and of course I went to Detroit to visit my parents and the rest of the family. I got home seldom, so I treasured the time spent with Mama and Papa.

Whenever I stepped out the door to go somewhere, Papa was ready to go too. Finally Mama took a hand.

"For goodness sake, S.T.," she said. "You can't go with Ollen everywhere he goes. He wants to spend some time with the young folks."

While in Detroit, I bought a new Mercury car. I shipped it

from New Jersey to Germany. When I returned to Munich, I hired a chauffeur. His job was to keep the car polished, drive the company commander and me to work, and take me to the clubs at night. I had my own special seat at one of the clubs.

Life was good.

In 1951, I went before the board for the rank of warrant officer, and passed. I asked to be sworn in, but I was informed there was an "excess of officers" in my field and I would have to wait. Was it racism? I had no way of knowing. There was still discrimination in the military, as elsewhere, but never blatant.

World War II opened more eyes to racism than anything else had. It equalized people and brought them together. It changed minds and educated people. It's been said that the integration of the military was a prelude to the changes that were later instituted in civilian America. Many of the racial fears and misunderstandings were challenged by President Truman's decision and the success of the military's program implementing it.

I was sitting at my desk one day when a white officer came by.

"Hey, Ollen," he said, "You black people are sure making your mark on the world. A guy by the name of Edward Brooke was just elected Congressman in my home state of Massachusetts."

Edward Brooke? He was in my outfit. Another black had made good. Brooke went on to be the first African American elected to the U.S. Senate by popular vote and served from 1966 to 1979. I thought of the men who had returned from the war and were making their mark on the world. I was proud of every one of them.

Then I thought of all those others—good men who had given their lives for their country. They never had a chance to prove their capabilities. As always, when I thought of them, I felt a wave of sadness.

In 1970, I returned with my wife and children to visit Hannelore's family as well as many places I had enjoyed while living in Munich. Our daughter, Kathy, was born in Ft. Lewis, Washington and our son had been only three years old when we finally left Germany, so naturally they couldn't know how Munich had played such an important role in their parents' lives.

We spent two weeks in Hannelore's hometown. Her brother, Helmut Geyer, his wife, Helga, and son, Rolf, had a large house with a big backyard with a beautiful forest nearby. We barbecued in the backyard every evening. We had barbecued ribs *In the field at Grafenwohr, Germany where I inspected a field kitchen. Circa 1950* and beer. It seemed like the whole neighborhood came.

I wanted to take Erich to see the hospital where he'd been born but couldn't find it. A policewoman pulled up to ask if we were lost. I told her where I wanted to go. She parked her vehicle, got in our car and showed us the way.

We visited Paris, Frankfurt, and Copenhagen and met some Italians, who were still very friendly to Americans. Because Europe was such a large part of our lives, Hannelore and I wanted our children to experience it. I think in the back of our minds, we hoped that they might someday make a prolonged visit there.

Part Seven
Civilian Life

Chapter 23
Fort Lewis

A few years before I was due to retire from the army; I began to consider my future. I liked Germany. I had lived in Munich so long it had become home.

Over the years, I had developed some close friendships with other military personnel and their families. I got to know quite a few Germans also, and had a good rapport with them. I knew I'd be able to operate a business successfully with the experience I'd gained in my military career and with the many contacts I had in both the army and the private sector.

The only drawback—and it was a big one—was the distance from my own family, especially between Mama and me. After Papa's death, it had become more and more important to me to be closer to family.

After so many happy years it was hard to leave Germany. Leaving Hannelore's mother, Kathe Geyer, was even more difficult. Hannelore and her mother had a very close relationship, and I loved and respected her mother the same as I did my own Mama.

Her mother—we called her *Omi* —doted on Erich, so it was a hard parting all around. We left with the promise that she would visit us often.

When Hannelore, Erich, and I boarded the train leaving Munich, the train station was packed with people—standing room only and people as far as I could see.

It looked like every German friend I had was there—and that was quite a few.

I was very surprised and deeply touched at the spontaneous display of affection by so many people I had come to care about.

I made an impromptu speech, expressing my feelings. It is the one speech I made in my life that I can't remember one word of. I guess I was too overcome with emotion but I do know I spoke with sincerity, affection, and gratitude.

An officer who apparently didn't know what was happening somehow worked his way within shouting distance.

"What's going on, Ollen?" he called.

"I'm going back to the States," I told him. "These people came to see me off."

"Well, my God, Ollen" he said. "I would have thought they were saying good-bye to at least a general."

As we pulled out of the station, people were calling, "Hurry back., Ollen. Hurry back." They were still waving as the train slipped out of sight around a curve.

When we arrived in the States, we spent a few days in New York visiting with friends from Germany until our paperwork was processed.

It was great to be back in the United States. We made a beeline for Detroit to visit relatives and friends. Hannelore and Mama hit it off immediately. Hannelore spoke perfect English so they had no trouble conversing. They were soon chatting like old friends.

Erich captivated everyone. He took his accordion along and played for the family. He loved that thing and was enthusiastic about squeaking noise out of it—what he thought of as music.

At two and a half he spoke only German, but he played contentedly alongside the other kids. They seemed to understand each other without words.

We visited, picnicked and caught up on old times and all the family news. Hannelore was surprised to learn I owned a rental property, which my sister had been managing while I was overseas. "I learned good money management from Mama," I told her. I didn't tell her that part of that learning came from a razor strap and part came from example.

The reunion was way too short for all of us, but that was all right. We knew we'd be able to get together for frequent visits as long as I was stationed at Fort Lewis, Washington.

When we left Michigan, we decided to take a different route

home so we could see other parts of the country. That turned into a tradition. We chose different routes, saw many interesting places, and met lots of friendly people over the years.

On one of our later trips, we met a rancher in Montana who invited us to spend a few days on his ranch, riding horses and enjoying whatever else the ranch had to offer. We would have loved that, especially the kids, but Mama was expecting us. We thanked him more than once for his generous offer. We never forgot him and he remembered us, too. At Christmas we received a beautiful card from him.

When my leave was over we bought a new car, a 1957 Mercury Monterey, and drove to Fort Lewis, Washington. When we arrived we were placed in temporary living quarters. It was almost a year before we got permanent housing.

At the time military pay was low. One day I found out from the personnel office that I had been overpaid when I left Germany. I was unaware of that and since I had a new family to support I took a job at the Officers Club. After a while things began to look brighter. I remember when I could save $25 in the bank each month, and that was a lot!

I was assigned to Fort Lewis Infantry Division Trains as mess steward, but the detachment had no mess hall in the garrison. We ate at the next one over, and my duties became administrative. The only time I operated the mess was in the field.

As first sergeant of the detachment with the Fourth Division Band, I had plenty to do. In fact, Fort Lewis was a very busy assignment. I attended many classes: Administration, Commissary Operations, Unit and Organization Supply, Quartermaster School, and Training and Methods of Instruction. A number of those classes were held in Fort Benning, Georgia. It was a great learning experience.

Also, I controlled the unit fund and had to approve all purchases and was on a lot of inspection teams. I had cooperation from everyone in performing these duties. I look back on my Fort Lewis experience as a challenging assignment and one I really enjoyed.

An exception would be field training. We often trained near

Yakima, Washington, where there was an abundance of snakes. I have always detested snakes. They were a big problem at Fort Huachuca during my basic training days. The thought of waking up in the morning to see a snake next to me would be enough to keep me awake all night. I always managed to find two trees close enough together so I could tie my cot up from the ground. Once I was in bed, I didn't get out till morning.

The guys who slept on the ground invariably woke to find two or three snakes sleeping alongside them. They soon learned to wake up without moving. They had methods for doing a quick kill before getting out of bed—anything from knives to pistols.

It's probably true that the snakes were hunting for a warm place to sleep and the GIs' body heat served that purpose, but I had to wonder where they slept when we weren't there.

—

The military is, by necessity, a very mobile way of life. I was sitting at my desk looking over some paperwork when I noticed a captain speaking with my commander. I couldn't place the man, although he looked slightly familiar.

He walked over. "Don't I know you?" he asked.

I had a flashback—the three Cs.

"Yeah," I said. "Boxtown."

"Those were good days," he said. "They gave me a good start for my military career."

We reminisced a bit. He was getting ready to go to France. *"I could use a good man," he said. "Would you like to transfer?"*

I shook my head. "I'm ready to stay stateside."

—

In 1962, a man who I understood was a member of the United States Congress came to Fort Lewis to conduct a survey related to equality and segregation in the military. He investigated my files and talked to many soldiers and officers in the division that knew me. That summer I was given a copy of the following letter written by Mr. Charles R. Cater, Attorney at Law, First National Bank Building, LaGrande, Oregon, on June 13, 1962.

Hon. Al Ullman
Member of Congress
Washington, D.C.

Dear Al:

On a recent visit to Fort Lewis, I met SFC Ollen Hunt, who, as I understand, is acting First Sergeant in Headquarters and Headquarters Detachment in 4th Infantry Division Trains now stationed at Fort Lewis, Washington. I was strongly impressed by this man's bearing, record, and abilities. I do not know him personally, and he has absolutely no idea that I am writing this letter. Men who serve with him inform me that he is, indeed, an exceptionally fine enlisted man, intelligent, fair, decent, and one of the hardest workers in the experience of those to whom I spoke.

I am sure that all of these qualities are well known to his commanding officers and fellow soldiers. However, what is apparently true is that he is serving undergrade and that in the job which he is commendably carrying out he is entitled to a rating of Master Sergeant, E-7. Sergeant Hunt has served in the United States Army for almost twenty years and is due for retirement this coming November. It seems to me that it would be fitting and proper that this man's country, for whom he has rendered those long years of faithful duty should recognize that and show its appreciation by elevating him to the highest noncommissioned rank—Master Sergeant.

I do not want to make a federal case out of this, Al, but I feel rather deeply that this man should receive the highest rating possible. Any small suggestions that might emanate from your office that would merely call to the attention of the powers that be the apparent oversight in the advancement of this man in grade would certainly be greatly appreciated.

Thank you, and with kindest regards and best wishes to you, personally, and to all of you,

> Sincerely yours.
> *Charles R. Cater*

I was overwhelmed by Mr. Cater's wonderful recommendation. Here was a busy man, a well-known man, who spent time and effort to draw attention to what he saw as an injustice to someone he didn't even know. The world would be a better place if we had more people like Charles Cater.

It's true; I was long overdue for an upgrade in rank. Head of promotions for food service said they had no record for my time served in Europe. They said, "When your records catch up to you, you may already be authorized for promotion."

My life in the service had been authorized step by step. I knew the records were available.

Disgusted, I wrote a letter to the head office in San Francisco. They sent me a packet of information and said, "You may already be appointed." I didn't know what that meant and I don't know if there was ever any follow-up on their part. However, soon after I received my copy of Cater's letter, I was summoned to Captain Easterday's office.

Easterday was a white man with piercing blue eyes. He looked at me like I was a specimen under a microscope.

"Sergeant Hunt," he said, "You've been recommended for promotion." He picked up my papers and quickly scanned them.

"It says here 'No Board Required,'" he told me, meaning that the promotion didn't need to go through the normal review process. "I want you to know I disagree with that one hundred percent. It's unfair to those who do have to go before the board."

I waited.

"We have an excess of officers," he said. "Those positions are frozen, so I have no authority to promote you or not promote you."

He dropped my papers on the desk.

"Dismissed!"

We both knew there were positions open. It was blatant racism. I was extremely angry.

I knew I could go over his head to Division Headquarters and get the promotion, but I didn't think I should have to fight for what I'd already earned. I had another option he could never have imagined. While in Europe, I had gotten to be friends with a one-star general's assistant. We often had coffee together. It turned out this man was a close friend to a cousin of President Truman. Apparently, the cousin had clout. "If you ever need a string pulled," my friend told me, "let me know. All I have to do is ask."

In the end, I followed the advice my parents had given me early in life. "Treat everyone with respect. Treat everyone as you want to be treated." Easterday had treated me with disrespect because of the color of my skin. I would not stoop to his level. I can't say I know what happened to Captain Easterday, whether he finally learned the hard way or the right way about what it means to love your country and respect its citizens. The only thing I knew was that I wasn't going to let him drag me down to his level. I would be nothing if I didn't follow the higher principles my parents had taught me.

I had already decided that if I got rank I'd stay in the military a few more years. If not, I'd retire. Sure, it made a difference in my retirement pay, but I was still a young man and I had every intention of having another career in the private sector.

On July 31, 1963 I retired from the army. After processing out, I went back to my desk and continued working. One of my clerks came over and in a low voice said, "I thought you were discharged today."

I was so accustomed to dealing with paperwork, I had returned to my usual duties, unmindful of the fact that once my discharge papers were processed, I was no longer in the military. After it was brought to my attention, I finished the day out anyway.

Chapter 22
A Civilian Once More

It was a peculiar feeling to go to bed one evening as a military man with twenty-one years of experience behind me, and then wake up the following morning as a civilian with no clear plan for the future.

For the first time, the next step in my life was not clearly marked. The transition from army to civilian life was abrupt. I was on my own.

I decided it best to treat the situation as an extended furlough while I considered career possibilities in the private sector.

We put the kids in the car and drove to Detroit. As always, I was thankful for my loving, wonderful family. We enjoyed being together and never ran out of things to talk about or things to do.

Our little daughter, Katherine, was handed from one pair of arms to another. Everyone liked to cuddle her. They enjoyed Erich's antics as well.

Hannelore and Mama had grown closer as the years went by. "Sometimes, I think you care more for Hannelore than you do me," I told Mama.

"Ollen, you're my son and I love you," Mama answered. "But Hannelore is my daughter."

Mama was in her seventies but she was as clear and direct as she'd always been. If she had an opinion, she expressed it, and she was generally right.

She told me about a recent trip to her doctor's office.

"Just because I was having a little trouble getting to sleep at night," she said. "The girls insisted I go." She rolled her eyes. "Ollen, you wouldn't believe what that man said."

"Tell me," I grinned.

"He said I should drink a little wine every night at bedtime. He started to tell me how much and I said, "Whoa, doctor! You can just stop right there. I have never touched a drop of any kind of alcoholic drink in my life, and I'm not about to start now."

That was Mama. She never compromised her principles in any way. If there was ever a woman who was religious and lived up to it, she was that woman.

She was content living with my sister and she wanted for nothing. I sent her money regularly while overseas. My sisters gave her money for birthdays, Christmas and such. Mama invariably tucked it under her mattress and forgot about it. At regular intervals, one of the girls would take out most of it and deposit it in Mama's bank account.

About the only thing she spent money on was upkeep for Papa's grave. Papa had been buried in Tennessee near the little country church that we had all attended for so many years.

―――

We had no time limit on our visit, but we knew we had a whole new life ahead of us—one we had to figure out for ourselves. I had my retirement, so I knew I wouldn't have to grab the first job that came along.

We visited friends in California, including Bill and Rita Bradley. All of us liked it there. I lined up a job through the Employment Office, mostly doing placement of food service workers. We found a house and began the process of buying it. When the temperature shot up to one-hundred degrees, we were told that was the normal temperature for the time of year.

That was it. I notified the employment office I wouldn't be taking the job after all, and we returned to Washington State.

I accepted a position as chef at Scotty's, an Italian restaurant in Tacoma. It was going well when someone told me a representative of Northwest Airlines had been trying to get in touch with me. I went and talked to the guy and learned Northwest wanted to hire me and they wanted me to work in Alaska. That was something to think about. After talking with Northwest's Seattle personnel, I was flown to Anchorage and met the staff there.

Incidentally, I never did find out who recommended me to

Northwest, but they already knew I had completed a course in international food preparation while in the three Cs. They also knew I had many years of experience in the military preparing foods from many countries. Airlines require international chefs, for they have to accommodate food preferences from many cultures. They made me a good offer. Hannelore and I talked it over and I decided to give it a try. We decided that she and the kids would stay in Tacoma for the time being and if the job worked out—well, she and the kids would follow me to Alaska.

Part Eight
Alaska

The Great Alaska Earthquake

On March 27, 1964, at 5:36 p.m. ADT (03:36 3/28 UTC) a great earthquake of magnitude 9.2 (moment magnitude) occurred in Prince William Sound. The epicenter was about 10 km east of the mouth of College Fiord, approximately 90 km west of Valdez and 120 km east of Anchorage. The epicenter was located at Lat. 61.04N, Lon. 147.73W., at a depth of approximately 25 km. This earthquake is the second- largest earthquake ever recorded. (The largest is a M9.5 earthquake in Chile in 1960.) The rupture lasted approximately four minutes (240 seconds).

The number of deaths from the earthquake totaled 131; 115 in Alaska and 16 in Oregon and California. Much of the damage and most of the lives lost were due to the effects of water waves. These were mainly of two kinds: the tsunami of open-ocean sea wave, generated by large-scale motion of the sea floor; and the local wave, generated by underwater landslides in bays of fiords.

The 1964 Alaska tsunami was the second largest ever recorded, again following only the one caused by the 1960 Chile earthquake (4 meters at Sitka). Of the 119 deaths attributable to the effects of the ocean, about one-third were due to the open-ocean tsunami: 4 at Newport Beach, Oregon; 12 at Crescent City, California; and about 21 in Alaska. Local waves claimed at least 82 lives. Maximum height reported for these waves was 70 meters in Valdez Arm.

The area where there was significant damage covered about 130,000 square kilometers. The area in which it was felt was about 1,300,000 square kilometers (all of Alaska, parts of Canada, and south to Washington). The four-minute duration of shaking triggered many landslides and avalanches. Major structural damage occurred in many of the major cities in Alaska. The damage totaled 300 to 400 million dollars (1964 dollars).

Excerpt text from Doug Christensen, PhD
Geophysical Institute, University of Alaska Fairbanks

Chapter 25
Earthquake!

I arrived in Anchorage about three weeks before the March 27, 1964 earthquake that made headlines around the world. Pots and pans rattled. Dishes crashed to the floor. Our huge coffeepot turned over. The floor shook under our feet. A quick look out the window showed cars bobbing up and down like they were on ocean waves. The floor we were standing on vibrated with more and more intensity.

"Earthquake!" someone yelled.

I wasn't sure what to do. When several employees ran down the steps, I went too. The vibration, grinding, and moving gradually died away.

Two cooks were pinned under some heavy equipment for two hours. Fortunately, they were not badly injured. There were no other injuries or fatalities in our facility.

Elsewhere in town, people were not so lucky. The J. C. Penney building, like many other downtown buildings, received extensive damage. One saleswoman was killed. The earth opened up and swallowed cars. Part of the bluff overlooking Knik Arm fell into the water, taking some homes with it. Miraculously, nobody there was killed. The damage was catastrophic, not only in Anchorage, but in many other areas of Alaska as well. An estimated 115 to 130 died, nearly all of them due to the tsunami that followed the quake. At the time, the earthquake registered 8.6 on the Richter Scale. Later it was upgraded to a 9.2 earthquake. You can still see where the earth dropped off between Third and Fourth Avenues in downtown Anchorage. People think it's just a natural hill but it wasn't there on March 26, 1964.

The earthquake left big fissures in the airport landing field.

Our building was no longer usable. We took up temporary headquarters on Elmendorf Air Force Base. That was our base of operation until the airport and our building were again ready for business.

I was impressed with the way Alaskans worked together to overcome the devastation and return things to normal. There was no looting and there were no other problems that often accompany such disasters. Everyone helped everyone else in any way they could. I have since realized that this is the Alaskan way.

I was ready to go home! I couldn't imagine living in a place where such devastation could occur. They asked me if I'd stay one more month. After one more month, and then one more month, I am still here in Alaska forty years later!

Chapter 26
A Career with Northwest Airlines

Working with Northwest Airlines was an interesting and challenging career. Anchorage is an international air crossroads, so our menus changed from flight to flight, depending on where the plane was coming from or where it was headed. I sometimes got special requests, like when British Airways first came to Alaska. If memory serves me correctly, I prepared the first Yorkshire pudding. The president of the airlines was on that flight and he was one of the first to taste it. I had always known British people to be very reserved, so you can imagine my surprise when the man wanted to hug me!

As far as I know, we never failed to fulfill a request for such special menus.

During the '60s, President Johnson and his entourage landed on Elmendorf Air Force Base to refuel Air Force One. We prepared meals for all of them. We were surprised and pleased when we later received a letter thanking us.

During my six years with Northwest, I progressed to head of food service. I liked my job. It changed from hour to hour. I was always busy.

In addition to my regular hours, I was always on call. If Northwest was notified of an unexpected incoming flight, they called me. I brought in whatever help I needed in the way of staffing and food and we got the job done. We not only produced in-flight meals, we also had a large cafeteria, buffet style. A lot of people were served there.

Northwest cared about its employees and showed it. They had banquets for their staff on special occasions and sometimes parties to recognize those who had done outstanding jobs. They gave certificates of appreciation and sometimes surprised an employee with a free meal in the cafeteria.

Working for Northwest was never monotonous. On one occasion, we received an overstock of shrimp. It was far more than we could use so I went on TV and advertised it for sale. I was excited about that. It was called "a shoot" and I was told the shoot went well. Maybe I should add "television personality" to my resume.

———

Northwest had flight kitchens in both Japan and Hong Kong. I was asked to go there and observe how they ran their operations and show them how to prepare some foods they were not familiar with. It was a sort of cultural exchange, where we could

learn culinary and operations techniques from each other. They paid for Hannelore to travel with me and furnished interpreters.

It was a chilly December in Tokyo but Japan has nothing to compare to Alaskan winter weather. The Japanese cab driver drove so fast it was frightening. At that time cars didn't have seat belts. I slid from one side of the seat to the other.

Northwest Airlines was noted for the many nice things they did for their employees. Ready to serve wine for an employee's wedding. Circa 1966

"Not so fast!" I said, hoping the cabbie understood English. He grinned. "All cabs very fast," he said. "No difference."

He didn't slow down. I held on and hoped for the best.

The people in the flight kitchen laughed when I told them about my dangerous ride.

"There is no such thing as a slow cab in Japan," someone said. "Amazingly, they don't seem to have many accidents."

The flight kitchen crew ran their kitchen efficiently. I made some suggestions and showed them how to make a few standard American dishes.

While I was out during the day, Hannelore amused herself by checking out the hotel. It had a lot to interest American travelers. In the evenings, we went sight-seeing. The architecture fascinated us.

After three days in Japan, we boarded our plane for Hong Kong. We had three days there also. The first thing I asked for was a slow cab.

Their flight kitchen also ran smoothly. They were doing a good job. I gave them some ideas for changes and demonstrated how I cooked a few things.

Hong Kong is a unique place. It is teeming with people twenty-four hours a day. There are people from all over the world, and every one of them is in a hurry. Hannelore and I held onto each other. We knew if we got separated in that crowd, it seemed like we'd never find each other again.

I think you could buy anything in Hong Kong. There's any kind of store there that you can imagine. People are also hawking merchandise on the streets with prices ranging from almost nothing to thousands of dollars.

It was interesting to listen to the various

Ready to cut the wedding cake. Circa 1966

languages and watch the constant flow of people in all manner of dress—some very colorfully attired. But it doesn't take long to tire of it.

We wanted to go sightseeing. Someone at the hotel told us we should see the paper houses. We stopped a cab. "Paper houses?" I asked. He nodded and opened the cab door. I later concluded he was used to that request. On a hill above Hong Kong stood cardboard shack after cardboard shack, a literal cardboard city. I stared. In my travels around the world, I had never seen people living in paper houses.

The cab driver was able to communicate to us that with every hard rain the inhabitants had to scavenge for more boxes and rebuild their crude shelters. It was a sobering sight. Billions of dollars changed hands in Hong Kong on any given day, and yet these poor unfortunates had no opportunity for adequate shelter. Their flimsy "paper houses" were dependent on the sun and at the mercy of the rain.

I have often thought of those cardboard shelters and their inhabitants. I have to remind myself that we in the United States haven't solved the problems of the homeless either. We also have people who live in boxes on the street and under bridges.

Asian food is good but I began to crave American food. Hannelore and I walked around Hong Kong hoping to find some kind of sign indicating American food. Unexpectedly we

Ready to enjoy the wedding feast. And the buffet is ready also. Circa 1966

found a place that had a rotisserie in the window with whole chickens revolving and browning. Oh, they looked good.

"This is it," I said and Hannelore and I went inside. When the waitress came for our order, I pointed to the one I wanted. She brought me the whole chicken and all the trimmings—American style.

"Can you manage?" she asked.

"You wait and see," I said.

When I finished eating there was only a pile of bones left. The waitress came back with the bill.

"You managed," she said, smiling.

We were invited to Christmas parties given by the hotel and the flight kitchen personnel. The language barrier didn't interfere with our enjoyment. Our hosts had the bands play some American songs for us. We found their music entertaining also. They were probably the most unusual Christmas parties we ever attended, but very pleasant with lots of good food and friendly smiles.

Chef, Ollen Hunt, for Northwest Airlines.

We gained a day when we flew to Japan. When we returned, we lost a day. It took a day or two to adjust and get in the mood for our own American Christmas.

I hired a number of people while employed at Northwest. One day a young man, Frank Lewis, walked in. Frank came from Bethel, up in northwest Alaska, and needed a job. He was a small man with no experience but willing to work. I decided to give him a chance.

I trained him as a dishwasher and he did a good job. Some time later we needed a busboy for the Sunday smorgasbord in our busy dining room, where we often served about a thousand people. He learned that job easily also. Frank worked hard and got along with everyone. He ending up working for Northwest for a number of years.

When I made the decision to leave Northwest and go into

business for myself, Frank said. "Ollen, be sure you save a spot for me."

———

I look back on my years at Northwest and can truly say they were happy times. I'm proud to have been a part of Northwest at that time because of what they did and how they did it. When they hired me they put their trust in my experience; when they saw what I could do they put their faith in my accomplishments. Even after I had left to work with Ken Haynes, I occasionally worked for them when they were in a bind. They called me once and said my replacement had not been fully trained yet. An unexpected flight was coming in. Could I come help out? I went. I called in the necessary help and got things moving. "Just stand back and watch," I told my replacement. "I'll show you how it's done." It went like clockwork. He watched everything that went on. Afterwards, I answered all his questions.

"I think I can do it," he said. "But it will be a long time before I can do it that smoothly."

Chapter 27
Hof Brau 1970 – 1993

While working for Northwest Airlines, I got to know a lot of people. I made some lifelong friends. Ken Haynes was one of them. I purchased vegetables and groceries from Ken, a vendor, who also owned a sandwich shop. He was interested in the restaurant business, as I was. While the J. C. Penney Mall was being built downtown, Ken kept me posted on what was happening. When the leases were available, he told me. "You know, Ollen," he said, "that would be an ideal location for a restaurant."

It didn't take long for us to become partners and sign a lease.

While my family and I went to Germany for a few weeks, the restaurant was built as Ken and I had agreed—modeled on the cafes I had frequented during my military career in Europe, with heavy beams on the ceiling and the décor in shades of brown. It was our plan to serve good food in a quiet, relaxed atmosphere.

We wanted to serve food that people couldn't get elsewhere. I suggested German food and Ken went along with it. Alaska has been a favorite destination for international tourists for a long time. Lots of German tourists as well as other Europeans come to Anchorage to get a taste of the "Last Frontier." I thought a restaurant serving German cuisine would be a perfect fit. And I know Americans enjoy international cuisine, too.

We settled on a name—"The Hof Brau." In Germany, *Hofbraus* are traditionally associated with a brewery, and some of them have an outdoor garden where customers can settle back with a beer, friends, and hearty food. Here in America, hofbrau-style dining means pretty much the same thing, except with an emphasis on the food rather than the beer. I envisioned a place that resembled the hofbraus I remembered from when I was stationed in Germany. I decided to skip the outdoor dining part since people don't seem too keen on dining outdoors in the typical Alaska winter!

I'd heard about a German restaurant in San Francisco so I flew down to check it out. I think it was also called the Hof Brau. They seemed to be doing well, although they were selling only lunches and sandwiches. I planned on a more complete menu, with a few choices of American food.

We opened the Hof Brau in 1970. Ken was a great partner. It wasn't long until he and his wife, Bobbi, and Hannelore and I enjoyed a social life together. Ken and Bobbi loved to dance. He liked what he called his "Texas music." I always asked the band to play some of his favorite songs.

When we opened the Hof Brau, we had two goals—to serve good food and give good service. All our meat came from Seattle, except for sausage, which was made fresh at Anchorage's

Alaska Sausage and Seafood Company. Everything on our menu was the best quality we could get.

We had a well-trained, dedicated staff. I hired people who wanted to work hard, earn a good living, and to contribute to making the Hof Brau one of the best restaurants in Alaska. It would take me too long to talk about their service and dedication, but a couple of

The hof Brau buffet and my meat carver are ready for hungry shoppers at the J.C. Penney Mall, downtown Anchorage, Alaska. Circa 1970s

them illustrate my point. Diane Hunt supervised the waitresses and workers on the line. She was chief cashier as well. She made it look easy. It was a pleasure to train her. She took every step to heart, and then trained everyone under her supervision exceptionally well. I must say that she was outstanding.

Another former Northwest Airlines employee I hired was Jackie Cerra. Jackie proved to be an excellent employee. She assisted me in producing new items for the menu such as salads, sandwiches, pies, and cakes. Her performance and ability were great contributing factors in the success of the Hof Brau.

Two more cooks, Bill Pearce and Les Pinion left Northwest and joined me at the Hof Brau. Although I had trained them somewhat at Northwest, they became good chefs at the Hof Brau. They also assisted me in other operations at the J. C. Penney Coffee Shop, Nordstrom's Shop, and the Sandwich Deck.

When I operated the Hof Brau, Sandwich Deck, the Nordstrom's Iron Gate Restaurant, and the J. C. Penney Coffee Shop, I employed a manager for each shop—Kathy, Jeane, and Martha. Having such excellent staff made my job much easier. Drawing from the managerial experience I got in the service, I taught them about business as well as about how I wanted our operation to run. The goal was to work together smoothly as a team.

I had not thought of running several businesses, but I was offered the Sandwich Deck, located in a little mall by the Captain Cook Hotel, then Nordstrom's Café. Next, I took over Penney's Coffee Shop. I added the glass bus stop and also ran the concession shop there.

The Hof Brau buffet, which I ran from 1970 to 1993.

In fact, I ran the whole building, except for selling bus tickets, and I took over as manager of the Penney Mall and the Alaskan Power Authority Building.

I had one store in the Penney Mall that had nothing to do with the food business—the Big and Tall Men's Store. It was probably the only shop in town that carried shirts that had sleeves long enough for me.

Running so many businesses at once sounds like a tough job. Managing all of the operations kept me on my feet for most of the day. It was helpful that they were all near each other in the downtown area and that I had an excellent staff to rely on.

But I took it all in stride: my career in the military had

prepared me well for it. One of my messes fed 3,000 troops three times a day, with seven serving employees. In the service, I acquired the skills to succeed.

I spent more time at the Hof Brau than at any of the other businesses. About a month after we opened, Frank Lewis, who used to work for me at Northwest, walked in wearing a big smile.

"Did you save me a spot in your new place, Ollen?" he asked. I started him on dish washing. After a few months, he asked me to teach him to become a chef.

I tried him on the buffet line, carving and serving meat. I felt he needed further training so I began teaching him in my office. When I thought he was ready, I moved him back to meat carving and he did well.

He really wanted to be a chef. He was willing and determined, but it was difficult for him, because he'd had no background in food service. I was strict with him and sometimes hard on him because I wanted him to succeed and I knew he would. I never let up although I sometimes had to step back and take a breather before resuming. After about six months, he could carry a shift alone. It was a proud moment for both of us.

Frank became a good chef and a valuable worker. He worked for me about twenty-five years, at both Northwest and the Hof Brau. Over the years, I considered him my right-hand man.

The Hof Brau drew lots of German tourists, especially in July and August, our prime salmon-fishing season. Our name was mentioned in Sweden, France, and other European countries, as well as in Germany. A lot of our foreign visitors would say, "So and so told us to drop in at the Hof Brau when we were in Anchorage." That's advertising you can't buy.

The Germans loved our food. Americans liked it too, but not as frequently. We soon added roast beef, turkey, and other standard American fare to accommodate the hungry downtown shoppers.

A group of about ten doctors came every year to hunt and fish. They were regular patrons for about fifteen years. They always notified me in advance, giving me the date and time of their arrival. They were great guys. I looked forward to their annual visit as I would with any friend.

One hunting season, one of them asked me, "Where's a good place for me to hunt a bear?" I pointed to a mountain in the distance. "You go on up there and hunt for a bear. I'll be here when you get back." I smiled, thinking, "If you get back," but I decided against saying it. No use in eroding his confidence.

—

When operating the Hof Brau, the Sandwich Deck, the Iron Gate, and Penney's Coffee Shop, I employed janitors to perform cleaning for all places after business hours. Over a period of time I had to change janitorial services because their businesses broke up or because they were not performing as required by their contract.

One day a lady came in and asked for an application. She was from an organization called the Kiva House—a group home for people with disabilities. I was happy to try to help them. They worked for me for a long time. One day their supervisor told me that they were having problems getting funding and they would have to shut down. One of the group, George Williams, applied to stay on with me and I approved, since he did a great job and was a hard worker, not only doing janitorial work but also taking on other responsibilities like helping out at the private parties we catered and collecting money at the door. He supervised the group, and helped them by promoting leadership when the program was failing. A trusted friend, George Williams would always be remembered as a good and understanding person. Once he came on board, George stayed with us until the Hof Brau closed for the last time.

—

After operating the Hof Brau for about a year, we decided to add a bar. As in other cities, liquor licenses in Anchorage weren't just created and issued. You had to buy an existing license. A local businessman wanted to sell his liquor license. We snapped that up. About a month later, Ken and I opened the Red Baron Lounge, which was attached to the Hof Brau.

We maintained a quiet and enjoyable atmosphere. It was a place where anyone could relax.

Soon we had more regulars than just the seasonal tourists.

Some people, individually and in groups, stopped by every day. One group of local women would come in once or twice a week to sit at their favorite table and enjoy beer and conversation. It was that kind of place.

We soon got most of the airline pilots who were in town on layover. Flight attendants from different airlines frequented the Red Baron also. One group of office workers, all women, came in often to chat and relax and just get away from the daily grind.

(upper) At the cash register and (lower) bartender and customers at the Red Baron Lounge, Anchorage, Alaska. Circa 1980s. (middle) The Bus Station, built in 1987, is in downtown Anchorage. I ran it from opening until 2001.

To the people who came there, the lounge was more like a social club than an ordinary bar. We served liquor and beer, soft drinks and food, but we never attracted the rowdy crowd or the hard drinkers. There were plenty of other places in town for them.

People liked to hang out there. Husbands passed time while wives spent money. There were many tempting shops in the mall, and the mall itself was central to all the major downtown department stores and offices.

People thought it was a good place to get together. The Alaskan Federation of Natives held their annual convention in Anchorage and we catered the food for their corporate meetings. We hosted many parties for the police department

The Sandwich Deck in downtown Anchorage, Alaska open for business—one of four food establishments I owned at the same time. Circa 1980s

over the years and sometimes we'd have a live band. We held dinners for churches as well.

Because of what I had learned early on from my parents and from what I had learned seeing poverty around the world, I knew that people would never be able to better themselves if they were hungry and living in the streets. Sure, some of them were there because of their own fault, but it gets hard to tell them apart from those who were destitute because of some personal tragedy. People will tell you I did my best to help those who needed a helping hand.

While operating the lounge, I employed several bartenders. They were all very nice to the people they served. One thing that I insisted on was that it would be a friendly bar where people could come to relax and the bartenders set the tone.

Lucille "Kuchie" Cole was one of my extraordinary bartenders. One day a person walked in the door and she realized he was drunk. She approached him and asked him to leave. Instantly, he knew she wasn't messing around. He left without a word. Over a period of time we had others come in, but the bartenders would always turn them around.

After about five years of running the businesses, Ken and Bobbi moved to Las Vegas. Later, they returned to Texas. Both passed away there. It was sad to lose such dear friends but we have good memories of two wonderful people.

I stayed even busier after I bought Ken out. I got as much pleasure from dealing with the public as some people do from hobbies.

Hannelore retired from her job at the Post Exchange on

Restaurant at the Iron Gate at Nordstroms in Anchorage.

Fort Richardson and was ready to tackle a business of her own. She bought the Before and After Shop from Bobbi. It specialized in maternity wear and baby clothes. It also was conveniently located in the Penney Mall.

I owned the Hof Brau and Red Baron for well over twenty years, the other businesses almost that long. Over the years, the staff and many customers became like family.

Chapter 28
Milt Odom – Anchorage Cold Storage

While employed at Northwest Airlines, I did business with many distributors and vendors. I got to know sales personnel at Anchorage Cold Storage. It wasn't until I opened the Hof Brau that I met the owner, Milt Odom.

Milt was a great guy, a very unusual person. I understand he began a business selling foodstuffs in Juneau, Alaska around 1932. He relocated to Anchorage in 1936.

In 1937, Milt acquired the franchise for Coca-Cola products for a dollar. I've been told he had a booth downtown where he mixed and sold it. The Odom Company still has exclusive rights to distribute Coca-Cola products in Alaska. What a deal!

Anchorage Cold Storage was, and is, a thriving business, one of the largest companies in the state of Alaska, and I know much of that success was due to Milt's hands-on approach toward his customers. For instance, Anchorage Cold Storage furnished the orange juice machine for my restaurant. I bought the orange juice from them and it was a pretty good seller year around. One day it quit working so I called Milt's manager. He told me he had no parts for it. I called Milt. A repairman walked in the door almost before I hung up the phone.

A few days later, I went down to his business for something else. Milt saw me and came out of his office saying "Hey! Everybody! Come here." Everyone within earshot dropped what they were doing and came to where we were.

"See this man," Milt said. "When he comes in here, give him anything he wants."

A large part of my restaurant supplies came from Odom's—

frozen food, liquor, meat, coffee, tea, spices—just about anything I needed.

Anyone who goes into the restaurant business can tell you that you might start making a profit in two years if you're lucky. Mostly, it's hard to break even. It takes a while to build up a clientele. It took Ken and me five years. In the meantime, when I was pinched for money, Milt extended credit. He trusted me. We had a handshake deal.

Over the years we became friends. He once asked me to start traveling with him. He was expanding his business across the Northwest and needed some help. It would have been a great experience, but I had a business to run and a family to look after.

Milt taught his boys to help run the business from the time they were big enough to help unload groceries, but never expected more of them than they were able to do.

Milt expected his employees to do a day's work for a day's pay. He paid well. His employees had more benefits than those working under a union contract and every one of them knew they could count on Milt if they had a problem.

The union tried to organize at Anchorage Cold Storage. I went down one day and they had a picket line set up.

"Don't cross the picket line," one fellow said. "We're here to unionize the workers. We'd like for you to respect that."

I know unions are very important to the American worker, but I felt it was more important for me to honor my friendship with Milt and to protect my business and the people I employed.

"The people at Anchorage Cold Storage are my friends," I told him. "I will buy from them as long as they are in business."

"We'll see," I heard someone say.

They put a picket line in front of J.C. Penney's to protest the Hof Brau's using Odom's products. While the picket line remained in place, Milt could not get any supplies from Seattle. The unions down there refused to ship his goods. Milt dealt with that in his customary "get it done" manner. He bought a ship and shipped his own goods.

He hired a lawyer from Washington, D.C. "There's no better way to spend my money than to spend it fighting the union," he said.

What the union people didn't seem to realize was that Milt

gave his people more than the union could ever ask for, so the employees would be paying union dues for nothing. After we took the legal steps we were able to have the picket line removed.

There are a lot of good stories told concerning Milt. Like the time he noticed some men sitting in the shade alongside the building.

"Those three guys outside there," he told his manager, "They're just wasting my time. I want them fired."

"Well, Milt," his manager said, "None of those men work for you. They're just waiting for someone to pick them up."

Milt shrugged. "It's their time, let them waste it."

Milt passed away about ten years ago. I still miss him.

———

He sure would be proud of his sons. They have continued the business, stretching out over the Northwest, and maintaining the integrity Milt demonstrated and instilled in them. All of them are committed to a company of service and lasting relationships with customers who become friends.

Beyond that, they are involved in many charities, donating both time and resources. And they never forget old friends.

A few years ago, Jimmie sent me a round-trip ticket to Seattle. A pilot flying a small plane took me from there to Oregon to what Jimmie called their cabin. I called it a hotel. It's a "rich people" area—mostly for higher-ups. Jimmie and a buddy golfed. They had another guest. He and I went sightseeing. We all got together in the evening for grilled steaks and lots of conversation. It was a wonderful time of relaxation and friendship.

Jimmie invites me every year. He is here in Alaska about once a month on business. Always in a hurry, unfortunately, but we usually have breakfast together and talk. I still take care of some things here for Jimmie.

Jimmie, John, and Billie are cooperative and wonderful people, as Milt was. They have exhibited the highest degree of professional knowledge and ability in this operation. Their dedication to their businesses and customers has been one of the most admirable it has been my privilege to encounter. And you can believe, over many years of operating businesses in the military and civilian life, I have known some of the best. They are a devoted family.

Chapter 29
A Lifetime of Service

Times changed: Anchorage was growing. Many people moved into the area, and with them came the new subdivisions and the suburban shopping malls that took away a lot of the downtown business we relied upon. People went to the malls to shop at the new chain stores and to eat at the popular franchise restaurants.

It's a story that has been repeated in many communities across America. Long-established local merchants are abandoned for national companies. In Anchorage, many downtown businesses moved or shut down. Tourism had changed too. Travelers were beginning to skip the Anchorage "hub" and instead went directly to their destinations on the Panhandle or to places in the interior such as Denali National Park. We had been in business long enough to witness most of the economic cycles that modernized Anchorage and we had weathered them all. But sometimes there are things that just come out of the blue.

In 1991, an elevator in the Penney Mall malfunctioned and a woman was killed. Because of this, in 1993, they decided to close the mall and all the businesses had to move. My wife relocated her business to the University Center. I closed the Hof Brau for good.

It was a sad ending for us after so many wonderful years, but it was a real tragedy for the family of the woman who lost her life.

———

When we closed the Hof Brau, it was a bittersweet time of reminiscing. It was also an opportunity to express my feelings to the loyal employees who had worked with me for so many years.

I gave Diane Hunt the following letter of appreciation and recommendation:

Upon your departure from this company, I would like to take this time to not only say thanks and good luck, but to point out a few important facts that occurred during your stay with the Hof Brau Company.

During my many years of food service I have not witnessed nor have I known a more loyal and devoted person. Your dedication to duty is the most complete one it has been my privilege to encounter and observe each day so closely.

Your constructive influence has instilled into many people of this company principles, character and moral traits, which add to every person's maturing and development. I was always both proud and grateful for your presence.

Your performance of duty as a chief cashier and supervisor ... has been a great contributing factor toward the success of this company. I shall always remember you as one of the finest qualities of person I have ever known.

I recommend Diane without qualification to any enterprise. I hope for your continuous success in all of your endeavors.

Thanks.
Ollen Hunt

When I closed the businesses, I kept the Bus Stop Stand. We had a lot of kids to deal with. Sometimes they came to me wanting a sandwich, but had no money. Sometimes they needed bus fare. I kept a tip jar and used the money to help the kids. I assisted some of them to find employment. I persuaded a few to join the military. They came back and thanked me later, without exception.

Many of the kids seemed to have no purpose in their lives. They just drifted along. That disturbed me.

One of the high school teachers invited me to speak to her students. I began to give speeches at the local high schools and encouraged the students to work toward a better future. I told them what a great opportunity I'd had in the Civilian Conservation Corps. I talked about the career potential with the military. My career evolved from my service to my country.

I always ended with my speech on "How to Progress." The students listened attentively, and asked questions afterwards. I gave each of them a copy of my speech, written when I was close to their age. Teachers requested copies. I had good feedback from both students and faculty.

I felt so strongly about the need for our young people to have a good future, I would sometimes stop loitering young people on the street and strike up a conversation with them. I once got into a discussion with three boys who said they were just hanging out. I told them how military life could start them on the road to a good career, that I had been successful in providing excellent food service in the government, corporate, and private sectors. And in doing so, I had traveled much of the world. I found out later all three of them had signed up!

Retired, except for the Bus Stop Stand, I became active in many worthwhile activities. Anchorage is a beautiful city. I remain willing to help in any capacity I can as a volunteer. I worked for the Board of Directors for the Anchorage City Parking Authority and served as a member of the Anchorage City Downtown Partnership. I remain a member of the National Chamber of Commerce based in Washington, D.C. I am also a member of TREA, a national association of retired people.

After retiring from the military I became very concerned about the eroding benefits of veterans. I never overcame the injury to my leg that occurred when the gas stoves exploded back when I was in combat training. I am now classified as 100% disabled. The military gives me a disability benefit and then takes that same amount from my retirement check. So I pay myself!

TREA, as an organization, invited veterans to write letters to them focusing on this gross injustice, and whatever else we might be concerned about. They planned to use these letters for lobbying purposes.

I sent letters to TREA and copies to President Clinton, my senators and congressman. Not surprisingly, I received no reply. Following is a copy of one of those letters.

3165 Campbell Airstrip Road
Anchorage, Alaska 99504
July 10, 1993

Mr. Al Ybanez
National President
TREA
P.O. Box 50584
Washington, D.C. 20091-0584
T3MO 3AE1

Dear Mr. Ybanez:

I entered the CCC about 1940 and remained there about 2 years. During my stay I attended several military schools, which also gave me the idea of doing something for my country at an early age. A few months after my completion, I was drafted into the army on November 22, 1942. I remained in service until July 31, 1963. When I retired, I left with the understanding that I had earned full medical benefits for life.

During my service I dedicated my life for the protection of my country and freedom. Each time I reenlisted I was required to take the oath and swore that I would serve my country and obey the rules, laws and regulations and also protect America to the best of my ability. I did just that.

I feel more than proud of my record., Because I came out with a clean and clear record, I feel proud to let anyone observe my record including the President of the United States.

Please allow me to speak for many other soldiers who protect our nation. They encounter hard training during the different phases. The front line tests them physically and mentally. No matter how bad I may tell any one it is, they cannot get the picture unless they have experienced it. Day in and day out being scared hungry and cold. Sometimes crying and praying! I could go on and on. However, protecting our nation's freedom becomes a part of your life; giving your life for the protection of every man, woman, and child of America.

I have occupied many positions while in service. Each one I worked very hard at and tried to make them better each day as follows:

Cook, Mess Steward: Consolidated Mess Operator, Food Instructor, Food Inspector, Administrator, Education Instructor, First Sgt, and several others.

Sometimes I felt that I was the best soldier in the service. I felt that my job was an great as the President of the United states. I also felt that if America trusted me and excepted my offer to offer my life for the protection of our nation's freedom I for sure wanted to be worthy of it and live up to my promise.

Now I find that someone feels that I do not deserve the full benefits that I was promised by America. They say there is a shortage of money and personnel. I never returned from the front lines and said I was shorty I remained there. I feel that God put every person on this earth to help each other in the manner that he desired and we as soldiers protected our nation to help every one.

I cannot understand the shortage in America. I understand that we pay people to plan in advance our living and way of ' life. I believe that they must stop and observe honesty and be fir to the people that they are working for. Perhaps the United States needs to again stop and observe the honesty of whoever disburses our funds to see if they are going to or getting to the place it is meant and to the people and areas it is meant to be; to the last and lowest hand. Our government after all, is meant for everyone.

Our colleges is one that we protected also. I wonder if they can come up with new ideas. A tighter and honest system is needed to demolish hate and teach the idea of helping and loving one another.

Upon my retirement, I opened up a restaurant for the convenience of the public in a downtown location. It went well for about twenty years and then a lawyer took over the management of the estate which led to the closure of my business after 23 years of operation. I contribute that to somewhere or somehow a dishonest act on their part. I should have had some one to turn to. This incident not only hurt me but many people of this city and it was not right.

I belong to several organizations since my retirement trying to serve and help my country. Each day I look to find ways to help an old lady across the street. That makes my day. We need peoples in government to increase not reduce the value of life just as I do, for the people who are paying his or her salary.

I feel that our government should be looking to find ways to increase our benefits and asking if there is anything they can do. For instance, I cannot understand a man who goes to jail for a crime who has full benefits when a soldier who gave/gives his life for the protection of his nation's freedom has limited benefits.

I could tell more and write on and on. To every soldier who gave his life for the protection of our nation's freedom I feel that our benefits should not be limited.

Sincerely.
Ollen Hunt

Cc: President Clinton
United States Congress
Senator Ted Stevens
Senator Frank Murkowski
Congressman Don Young

Part Nine
Family Memories

Chapter 30
My Wife and Children

Hannelore

I met my future wife Hannelore in November of 1948 one evening in Nuremberg. I was out driving around and a beautiful girl was walking down the street with and arm load of books. In order to make contact I stopped my car and asked her for directions to the Post. Naturally I knew the way, but this was the perfect reason to start a conversation. I found out that she lived close by and was on her way home form classed at a private business college. She lived with her retired schoolteacher aunt while going to school. Her mother and brother lived outside of Nuremberg.

Since I knew the time she was on the way from school, a couple days later I waited to meet and talk to her again. We make a date to go to the movies on the weekend. Germans at this time had no problems with a black American dating a white German girl. We found out that we had a lot to talk about and both liked to go to the movies. I had a '47 Chevy and many times one of my friends and his girlfriend would go with Hanna and me on trips together. We especially liked to go to Munich where I was stationed earlier. There I had a lot of friends that we visited

In 1951 I had to return to the States and was stationed at Aberdeen Proving Ground. It was very hard for me to leave Hanna and Germany. When I returned to Germany I was once again stationed in Munich. It was a few hours drive on the Autobahn to Nuremberg, so a year of so later we decided to buy an apartment in Munich and submit our papers to get married. Hanna worked for EES headquarters in Nuremberg and got a transfer to Munich. Getting married was no simple matter. Her parents and relatives accepted me very well and did everything to help us. We got married twice - once in the morning by the German Registrar and again in the afternoon in the Henry Kaserne Chapel by a Methodist chaplain. The only sad experience of the day was with the chaplain. He was a Southern Baptist and said it was against his belief to marry a mixed race couple. He had us sign an acknowledgement that we could not live below the Mason-Dixon Line once we were married. However, all her family and friends attended and it turned out to be a wonderful day. We've been married more than fifty years now.

We were very lucky as a month later the marriage law changed and instead of having to leave the country to the Stated within 6 months of our marriage, we were able to stay in Germany. Our son was born in Munich and later our daughter was born in the United States.

Erich

Our son was born on December 30, 1954, in a hospital in Munich, Germany. We named him Ollen Erich Hunt, but we've always called him Erich to avoid the confusion of both of us having the same first name. He was a wonderful child. I knew that as soon as I looked at him and I've never had reason to change my opinion on that.

Hannelore and I had been living in an apartment, but once I got authorization, we moved into military housing. We had three bedrooms so there was plenty of room, even with all the toys and other baby accessories.

Several German ladies in the neighborhood had gotten to know us, and they'd often come over to see if they could put him in the stroller and push him around the neighborhood. With all the attention he was getting from the neighbors my wife on occasion had to say "NO" - so she could enjoy him. He sat in that stroller, looking around with his big eyes. You'd have thought he was a miniature king.

Erich was a very alert, active child. When he was about two and a half years old, I bought him an accordion at the PX. He and I would play with it, which is not to say we were musicians. I thought of him as my little music man. Sometimes I would play it with him, then throw my hands up and say - "See the greatest music man from Deutschland." We had fun with the accordion. When we were transferred back to the United States in 1957, he made sure he had it with him. I had a thirty-day leave. Hannelore and Erich had never been to the United States. We stayed in Detroit with my mother, other family members and friends. He could not speak much English, but he could play with the other children. They had a good time together.

Our first visit home was one of many. Each year when I got leave, we drove back to Detroit to spend time with family, relatives and friends. I don't know who looked forward to it most, Mama of Hannelore.

In a conversation with Mama, I said, "You're talking as though you like Hannelore better than you like me." Mama answered that real quickly. "She's your wife and my daughter and I love her." I knew Mama loved me. She'd have told me if she didn't. So I let it go at that.

Erich went to kindergarten at Fort Lewis Elementary School and finished the second grade there when I retired from the service in 1963. We moved into a big green stucco house at 7649 South Pine St. in Tacoma. Sometimes I think we should have bought that house. It was surrounded by tall hedges and stood next to a large field overgrown with blackberries and crab apple trees. The kids had fun playing in the field and enjoyed what was then a kind of rural setting—farms and horse stables—even though we were by no means in the country.

Erich and Kathy would bring back bags of blackberries for pies, pancakes and just eating. Erich went to Arlington Elementary School from third grade to the beginning of fifth grade. How could I have known when I retired that in less than two years I'd be in Alaska working to move my family up north? I went up alone on my Northwest job at the airport, getting up there in plenty of time to experience the Good Friday quake. The family moved up in the fall of 1965.

The house we settled into was in the Mountain View area of Anchorage on Mumford Street, so Erich went to Mountain View Elementary a little after the beginning of his fifth grade. The kids seemed to adjust pretty well to the change in scenery and climate, even though as you can imagine, it's sometimes hard for kids to leave familiar faces and surroundings. Washington was a beautiful state, full of forests and mountains and waterways. Alaska had all of that too, but it had one more thing: a real winter with snow! Erich, Kathy and their friends found plenty to do in the winter, playing in the snow, sledding, skating, and staying out until they'd come home half frozen. The cold season would bring the animals down from the hills, so some mornings you'd wake up to see a moose or two chewing on the paper birch trees right outside the window. It was a great place for the kids to get to like fishing for salmon and being in the outdoors.

In moving from Tacoma to Anchorage, Erich was far enough ahead in his studies to be asked by his fifth grade teacher to teach the class about the math subjects of area and perimeter. He did very well at school. Around that time, my wife had arranged for Erich to take violin lessons with Mr. Gorsuch, a violinist with the Anchorage Symphony, with whom he studied for about a year. It was in the sixth grade that he started playing guitar, thanks to his best friend at the time and to his sixth grade teacher who'd bring his guitar to class for sing-a-longs. I can remember many days and nights of hearing Erich play his guitar behind the closed door to his room.

When Erich joined the local Little League baseball team I coached his team for a couple of years. He was good at playing ball and we had a great time at every game and every practice. On one occasion while I was out of town, Erich pitched a perfect shutout. He could hardly wait for me to get home, so he could tell me.

It was always fun whether we won or lost, but when we won we'd all pile into cars an go to A&W Root Beer for ice cream, sodas and other "nutritional" food as our reward. Not every parent has the energy or can take the time to do voluntary community work like coaching baseball, so I feel fortunate that I could do it for my son and for the kids. All of children, adults, learned about teamwork and striving toward a goal, and I hope that some of the things that I helped the kids to discover made them and us better people later in life.

Erich tells me that one of his main reasons for wanting a job was so that he could buy a bass guitar. Through my business contacts I got him a part time job with Carrs supermarket store. Carrs had a program where they'd award scholarships to promising employees going to college. Apparently, Erich did well enough at his work and in his scholastics because he was awarded two scholarships and got his picture in the paper. We were very proud of him. Soon he picked up a bass and was playing in rock and blues bands but he said he found what he was looking for in jazz pretty early in his music career. He has played it all these years.

He attended Alaska Methodist University and the University of Alaska in Anchorage as a psychology major before transferring to the University of Southern California and majoring in English Composition. He also took music theory, music history, and music performance classes. He was active in the black student union at USC and one year chaired the Black History Month activities program.

He had a good deal with Carrs. When he was home between semesters, he could work any shift he chose.

After Erich came back from college in 1977, he started playing all over Anchorage at clubs and restaurants like Elevation 92 and the old Monkey Wharf, concerts at the college, and wherever a talented bass player was needed. He scored and performed a multimedia production called *Dreamer and the Dreamed*, and recorded for film scores, music demos and commercials including one for the first cable company in Anchorage. He also worked with me for a while, doing paperwork for my business. He and some friends formed a band and played a New Year's Eve party at the Hof Brau. I overheard many positive comments on the music.

He stayed in Anchorage for about a year and a half. His girlfriend at the time used to live in Honolulu before coming to Anchorage to work at the Alaska Repertory Theater. Their paths crossed at Elevation 92. Erich tells me that she decided it was too cold in Alaska and invited him to join her there. He says that he didn't decide to go right away, but a few months after she left Erich approached me. "Dad, I'd like to got to Honolulu for a month."

"When did you plan to go?" I asked.

"This evening."

I got on the phone and arranged for a ticket. I took him to

the plane. He took a suitcase and his electric bass with him and says he found work immediately. I knew it was going to be an extended stay when he asked me to ship his double bass to Hawaii. A good friend of his helped me to build a big plywood shipping container that looked like Frankenstein's coffin. After a lot of work we shipped it off. When he called me later and thanked me, he told me that if push came to shove he could always live in that box.

The month-long stay stretched into seven years that he said included clubs, conventions, recording and concert engagements. When work got slow in town he worked on the inter-island cruise line in the ship's orchestra. Besides the sun, sand and sea breezes, he said one of the highlights of his stay in Hawaii was touring to Japan in 1984.

He met his wife Karen in 1983. She was teaching at the University of Hawaii at the time. They fell in love and lived together for the rest of his rather long Hawaiian vacation. They moved to the Bay Area, with Karen working as a lecturer at San Francisco State and Erich, working as legal temp by day and musician by night. They got married in the fall of 1989. We came down for the reception and it was there that we met Karen's brothers and sisters and their families. It was a very moving reception and we had a wonderful time getting to know each other in such a beautiful area of the country. Karen is now a professor in the Speech Communication department at SFSU, a noted scholar and academic. Erich works as a paralegal at an energy company in San Francisco by day, but at night, the boy I once called the "greatest musician in all of Deutschland," is still playing music.

A Daughter's Memories - Katherine

As far back as I can remember my Dad, I remember a tall, big man. I remember my Dad coming home for lunch and taking a nap with me. I always liked to put my feet in his army boots just so I could be a soldier like him. My Dad worked some side jobs so I didn't see too much of him. After growing up, my parents would always tell me it cost 25 cents for a loaf of bread.

I remember my father when we would travel from Washington to Michigan. My brother sat directly behind my father in the car and I would sit directly behind my Mom. I think I had the advantage because it was a little harder for my Dad to sway me than my brother. But my father always instilled family into us. We would visit our aunts, uncles and cousins. Over the years my father made sure I got to know the wonderful people they were.

Before I go any further with that, I have to tell you the part when we were living in Tacoma. We lived in a huge green house that had hedges all around. I was about five or six years old. There were garter snakes. I was so afraid of the snakes I wouldn't go outside. Well, my big, tall Dad would take care of that. My Dad would hit a couple of snakes and I would feel so safe. I felt like my Dad was my hero. Well, as I grew up and heard some of his childhood story, I came to find out that Dad was just as afraid of those snakes as I was! But that's okay, he was still my hero.

From about that time maybe a year passed and my Mom told me we would be moving to a place called Alaska—Anchorage, to be exact. I had no idea where we were going, just that they had a lot of snow. I was happy about that.

My father had accepted a job with Northwest Airlines as the in-flight chef. This part was great because each time we went on vacation, we got to fly first class. Back then we got little slippers, glass salt and pepper shakers, a face towel that has hot and lemon smelling and received a lot of attention from the stewards. Oh, those were the days. Now you're lucky if you get food on the plane.

Anyway, growing up in Anchorage was probably one of the smartest things my parents could have done. It was not a large city and we didn't have a lot of bad things to influence us. I do remember my Dad saying; "Make sure the doors are locked." He'd also say be careful of people that would call you friends right away. Once again my Dad instilled family. As I've grown older, what my Dad was saying is true—your family is your backbone.

I can also remember a special time when my father had the Hof Brau. I remember eating lunch with him and a homeless person came up and asked my father to buy his carving. My father wasn't interested in the carving but asked the man if he was hungry. The man said 'yes' and my Dad told him to get in line and get something to eat. I was so proud to see my Dad lend a helping hand to someone who was less fortunate than he was. My father seemed so stern. My father has a big heart and he tries to help others as much as possible.

As I've gotten older, my father talks a lot about the war and what he has done in the military. I sit there in amazement, because I couldn't even begin to picture myself in some of those situations. My father has served the military and his community very well. When people talk about my dad they always have wonderful things to say and how they miss him so.

Chapter 31
A Final Word

I have been blessed with opportunities to progress in my thinking and actions since that day in my childhood when I gave my first speech. I have advanced in my career since it began, and pursued more learning and education as well. I received my GED in the military, plus many other certificates of learning, but I never attended college. Both my children did. Erich received his degree from USC and Katherine's was from Western Michigan.

Someone asked me if I regretted not having gone to college. "Absolutely not!" I said. "I wouldn't trade the education I got in the service for any number of years of college. The military is an education in itself.

"I have been successful in providing excellent food service in the government, corporate and private sectors.

"I have had fifty to seventy-five employees at one time and helped them all to progress in their career choice.

"I have employed people from various cultural backgrounds and countries and I have provided employment for the handicapped.

"During my career I have kept abreast of administrative laws, which often change, and have always maintained specific, accurate records.

"If I had any more education, I wouldn't know what to do with it!"

Unto those who talk	Help look after your fellowman
And unto those who go	Help him to continue on
The steam that blows the whistle	Love him with all your heart
Shall never turn the wheel	And lift with all your might

Ollen Hunt

Afterword
My Father's Book
by Erich Hunt

I was surprised and delighted when my father told me he was going to write a book about his life and about his years in the army. After he retired from the businesses that took up the whole of his day, I was a little worried about what he would be doing with himself with all of that free time. Other people look forward to their retirement years as a time to finally do the things they could never do while working, things like hobbies, pet projects, community volunteering, and travel. And even though my father was an avid little league coach when I was in the game, I had never known him to have the typical "after-I-retire" interests outside of his work. No rose garden to nurture and protect against the inevitable hordes of garden pests, no old cars to restore to cherry condition in a tool-laden garage, no miniature trains to run around an elaborately landscaped track, no furniture to build once the vocation-fettered carpenter is freed to pound away to his heart's content.

Even though my father appreciated the value of books and literature (an appreciation of which he made sure my sister and I were aware) I can't say I expected him to start reading the Great Authors on Day One of his retirement. I don't ever remember seeing him read a novel cover to cover. So, when he told me he was going to put his story to words I couldn't have been more surprised than if he told me he was going to write a symphony or paint the next Mona Lisa.

Being an overly cautious and worrisome person, I immediately started thinking about obstacles, roadblocks and detours he might face in making this a reality. Writing an autobiography has got to be a painful, delicate project. How many of us could sustain the drive, the will and the introspection required to sift through "a lifetime of learning" and produce a book about themselves that reflected who they were and who they have become? A book that, through the process of writing it, forces the writer to sift through dim memory to recapture the good times and the bad times as they really were. How many of us could succeed in producing an autobiography that wasn't filled with self-inflated fiction?

I'm afraid I did not inherit much of my father's sense of direct action. In face of a large task I proceed incrementally, calculating my approach, analyzing the obstacles, constantly checking wind and weather. I rarely get anything done. My father decided to write a book and, with the help of his friends, family and other capable advisors, proceeded straight through to the finish line. The book you are now reading is a testament to his sense of direct action, a sense that you get a feel for in the way he recounts his life in these pages. On top of everything else I've learned from him, this is just the latest and, perhaps, his most important lesson.

From the time that I was first able to get a sense of who I was as an individual, I grew up believing that I was quite different from my father. And given that I grew up under circumstances that could not have been more different than his, it is only logical that our approaches to life (direct action versus analytical stalling) would be somewhat divergent. But as if to illustrate that the apple doesn't fall far from the tree, a funny thing happened to me one day a long time ago, back in college. I was ambling down a street, absent-mindedly glancing into store windows when the sunlight and shadow and the angle of the glass played with my reflection just so, and I saw for a brief but illuminating moment my father's face, his stance, his shape, his way of walking. I am my father's son and, as he mentions in this book, he is his father's son.

I am also my mother's son, and although the focus of this book is my dad's military years, I would have been a little more comfortable with a greater inclusion of my mother's story, her childhood in Germany, how my mother and father met and lived together in Europe, how they sustained their marriage and raised a family through uncertain times and across two continents. I can't imagine how my father could have gotten through all of this without her love, sacrifice and support.

Furthermore, I wish he would have included more of his life in Alaska although he does cover some of the great things he did. He was one of a handful of successful African-American business people in the city and that was a mark of distinction all by itself. A lot of people got to know him and they were always coming up to me telling me how much they liked him and how good the food was.

I guess this will all have to be in the next book.

Below is a discussion of some of the background issues I hope will help give context to what my father relates through the lens of his personal experience. I leave out the sources I consulted in the process of fact-checking the particulars he mentions. There are now many websites and books dedicated to the topics I merely touch on here. In terms of American History and especially as concerns the Armed Forces, a good place to start is the Veterans Administration and the National Archives in Washington. D.C.

My Father's Story as an African-American Oral History

My father's story covers a lot of ground, stretching from the tumult of the turn of the century, the Great War, Great Depression, World War II, to the emergence of the United States as a bona fide World Power, and up to the present age. Many threads of history weave themselves through the narrative here and students of history will understand how they provide context to his experiences. My father's life as an African-American, and as an African-American soldier during the war years is especially significant because 1) not many people know about the domestic issues at play in America during World War II beyond its widely-known geopolitical dimensions, and 2) not many people are at all aware of the monumental struggles that took place in the political and military arenas of American society that resulted in the black soldier's "right to fight" for the democracy that he believed in, for the people he loved, and for country of his birth.

Although some African-Americans had prospered as a result of the changes wrought by post-Civil War Reconstruction and the Gilded Age of American capitalism, most understood all too well that they were living in the shadow of the "strange system of Jim Crow." The turn of the century had already seen the rise of the corporation, the factories of the Industrial Revolution, and the concomitant assertion of labor movements. The waves of new immigrants who arrived in America during this time by their very presence challenged mainstream America's sense of itself, and racist sentiments that had previously been reserved for blacks and Native-Americans now were applied with renewed vigor against those arriving here voluntarily. Indeed, there was a time when the Irish and the Italians were considered nonwhite. Despite the virulent anti-foreigner legislation and vigilante action (e.g., the history of the Chinese and Mexican workers in the Frontier West is especially harrowing) that shared its xenophobic aims with groups like the Klan, some immigrant groups found themselves moderately accepted and assimilated into the mainstream, and for both economic and sociological reasons, took on, among other things, the mainstream's animosity toward the black Americans already here. Several great waves of rural southern blacks coming to the North to escape the closed system poverty of the South, put the questions of racial co-existence and American privilege on the front burner in many northern cities. Operating as a counter force to Industry's exploitation of the working class, the labor movement's many strikes and protests prompted factory owners to find more pliant workers to keep the economic engine going, whether in the steel mills of the Northeast, the sugar and cotton mills of the South, or in the stockyards of Chicago. The labor movement and its striking workers were hardly pleased to see rural blacks being shipped in to take their places on the assembly line.

Into this cauldron (by no means limited to the labor arena) newly settled blacks established communities and conducted life as they could, and within their proscribed boundaries, found a life somewhat better than the monocultures of the South.

Unfortunately, by the time of my father's birth, the tempo of violence toward blacks had increased along with the burgeoning, mobile population. A legacy of brutality, lynchings and mob action filled the evening newspapers, and the terrorism (as we now would call it) was conducted by an entrenched, privileged, racist mentality primed with long-standing animosity, buttressed by the social and "scientific" philosophies of its institutions, and prompted to action on the flimsiest of excuses. Later in the century, one can be sure, the authors of the modern 1950s and 1960s civil rights struggle we have only now canonized came of age with the memories of East St. Louis, Philadelphia and Houston (1917), the Red Summer of 1919, the Greenwood riots in Tulsa (1921), Harlem (1925) and Detroit (1943) fresh on their minds.

Civilian Conservation Corps

Franklin Roosevelt's election and the New Deal were a direct result of the economic trauma of the Great Depression. The Civilian Conservation Corps (CCC) served the needs of a large, unemployed population and rehabilitation of the nation's infrastructure that had either not been developed or that had been ravaged by over-exploitation and expansion. With a vast labor pool to organize and a large territory to cover, the government give the task of the logistical and organizational implementation of the CCC to the Army. By the time my father signed up, the CCC had a decidedly military flavor. Support for the corps was not unanimous: for instance, the US Labor movement worried that this was a harbinger of the eventual regimentation of the national workforce, but over time most of the country regarded the CCC and the New Deal as correct fixes for an economically dysfunctional nation.

In the beginning, the CCC was not set up to offer the types of educational and vocational training my father mentions; these features were added later on as the program gathered steam. There seems to have been an initial focus on the unemployed of the Industrial North, but soon enough the workers included rural blacks like my father, whose communities benefited from the wages sent back home by the now-gainfully employed. The history of the CCC and its accomplishments are well-documented and forms a fascinating chapter in pre-WWII American history.

Since the CCC projects were spread across all of the states and territories, the recruits were shipped and stationed far and wide. For many rural blacks like my dad it was the first time they had left their local communities, and if they didn't decide to permanently settle in the host communities, the workers returned with stories of their experiences at the far-away camps. For the communities that hosted the camps, the CCC proved a mixed blessing. Local businesses were suddenly made viable again with willing, salaried customers; the local constabulary were kept busy policing a larger populace; and the town and community leaders were alarmed and, in some cases, appalled by the sudden presence of a noticeable contingent of black workers in their midst.

The rise and fall of the CCC, which many regarded as a temporary rather than a permanent program, had to do with several internal and external factors. The state quota system used to populate the ranks was changed with successive bureaucratic leaderships, and political infighting regarding patronage undercut the altruistic nature of the New Deal programs including the CCC. Election year budget-cutting reduced the vigor of the program. With more people going back to regular work thanks to the national economic recovery, and the industrial stimulation generated by the winds of war in Europe, the CCC was drained of its prospective labor pool. After so much accomplished, the CCC, established by the Emergency Conservation Work Act of 1932, was defunded and closed out in 1942.

African-Americans in the Armed Services

African-Americans had participated in this country's wars since its inception, but their presence was always as a segregated, militarily inferior, auxiliary force and this segregated regime was not fully extinguished until the Korean War in the 1950s. The post-bellum reorganization of the US Army in 1866 established the colored 9th and 10th Cavalries, which later became known as the famed Buffalo Soldiers. The black troops who were eventually employed on the Western Frontier earned their honorific name around 1871 from the Comanches who were sufficiently impressed with the stamina and trail skills of the black soldiers. The Buffalo Soldiers participated in the expansionist Indian and Mexican Wars as well as providing U.S. protection for wagon trains, mail routes and other national assets. They played an important role in the Spanish American War at San Juan Hill and in the Philippines.

In the Great War (WWI), African-American troops went

overseas to Europe where their battle experiences—and their segregated status—foreshadowed some of the things my father talks about during his WWII service a few decades later. On the domestic scene, among those who fought against the laws (and against the mobs) during the post-WWI racial disturbances were former black soldiers who were freshly empowered by their European experience. Thanks to the Armed Services they had glimpsed another way of life while over there.

There was much heated debate about the role of black soldiers during the run-up to America's entry into WWII. The forces at play in the larger society came into sharp focus as the country geared up for the hostilities that broke wide open for the US with the attack on Pearl Harbor. Black America—if it was to commit itself to the military—was well aware of the irony of fighting against a racial ideology, and dying for the liberation of others, that African-Americans were denied at home. The famous "Double V," victory abroad and victory at home, was shorthand for the hopes blacks pinned on their demonstration of patriotism for a country resistant to the sincere application of its own creed.

From the beginning ,and even later on when the war's attrition and casualties made it clear that all hands needed to be on deck, the military was adamant about maintaining a segregated force. Blacks, like my father, were relegated to support roles, their movements, transfers, theaters of operation, and their command structure was tightly controlled. The black officer corps was a perfunctory appendage to the fighting force: black officers were not to command white troops; medical staff was segregated and billeted accordingly. It is startling to realize that the blood plasma supplies for the war wounded was not officially "integrated" until December of 1950.

The hostility from the brass and from the white soldiers must have felt like a cruel joke to the Buffalo Soldiers like those in my dad's outfit, the 92nd. There were many instances of racial abuse that had to be endured even as the bombs were exploding all around.

Conflicting orders, the fog and chaos of war, the intentional placement of black troops in untenable combat positions—when white troops failed in their missions, the formidable

German Wehrmacht was to blame; when black troops failed it was read as an indictment of their dedication and an indication of their incompetence in the art of warfare. They were branded cowards, deserters, etc. With notable exceptions in central European Theater, black soldiers were skipped over for training in heavy artillery and tank operations because they were said to be constitutionally incapable of handling heavy machinery; their reflexes were just not fast enough(!).

Seeing that making progress with the Army's policies was going to be a long haul, the civilian and government black leadership tried for a fresh start with the newly formed Air Force, but the Secretary of the Air Force was not budging. Some saw the establishment of the pilot program at Tuskeegee as a capitulation to the segregated regime that permeated the Armed Forces. The Secretary of Navy, ostensibly responsible for the conditions leading up to the Navy's Port Chicago tragedy, suggested that policy changes regarding desegregation should be placed in the wastebasket.

There were many reported and unreported instances of the heroism and bravery of the black troops; more than most, they knew what they were fighting for and what was at stake. Like other black outfits, the 92nd was much decorated.

Even so, as my dad mentions, all of the soldiers learned about the equality of the foxhole and the equal opportunity of the bullets heading in their direction. The proximity to black troops provided white soldiers with a heightened respect for their black comrades and it is easy to assume that not few of them returned home after their tours with a different attitude about black people in general.

My dad never regaled me with his war experiences; never boasted to me about this or that battle. In fact, much of what he writes about his time in Italy and Germany is brand new to me. Reading up on the war and the Army and life in the States at that time, and I'm mystified that he didn't include more of his own personal challenges dealing with the social issues of the day, especially those that emerged after the war. As you can see he has taken a more magnanimous approach to these issues than I would have but I take him at his word that he has made a kind of peace with the past. He did his best to survive and leaves the rest to Providence.

My Folks

Coming back to the States with a German wife and a bi-racial baby must have raised some eyebrows, must have been cause for some friction with the segregated world that was slowly, inexorably, legally dismantled in the late '50s and '60s. The Armed Services, so intransigent previously, had evolved to the point where some saw it as being a model for civilian life. People were saying that if it worked in the service, it could work in the general society.

Many black servicemen had returned home to the States with heightened expectations about what kind of country they wanted to live in. Many chose to stay in Europe because they found a respect and openness they couldn't imagine in the States.

Some number of black servicemen came back with foreign-born brides. While we were stationed at Ft. Lewis, a lot of my early childhood friends (including my first real crush) were bi-racial and the Haydens, the Vasons, the Johnsons, the Taylors were all great people just like my folks. Tom and Lori Hayden were my godparents, and thanks to Bandmaster James Taylor, I got my first up-close look at a doublebass.

Growing up in Washington state and then in Alaska, it took a while for me to figure out who I was in a world that seemed to covet conformity and homogeneity. Identity struggles are typical enough in children—mine had an added twist. I gradually lost my primary language (German) and had a quintessentially '60s American upbringing. Both my parents provided my sister Kathy and me with the fruits of their respective cultural heritages and values and as result I learned early on the type of harmony that seemed to be missing from the roiling world just outside the door. I think of them as being a part of the vanguard of the still sought-after multi-racial, diverse American society that had its seeds in the tumult of WWII. I love my father and mother dearly. They are more extraordinary than they will ever admit.

Final Note

Finally this book could have only come about through the help of the Veterans Administration and its efforts to get veterans to contribute to an oral history program, chronicling the personal stories of those in the Armed Services. Much of what we know about war is through the eyes of those who have been there to witness it first hand, the combatants (some like my father) and the civilians caught in between. These personal narratives help to reaffirm what is good in life, what one has learned; they help to articulate what we value.

But Time heals and hides memory. It eases the pain of long ago, or it reshapes the memories to fit what might have been. Time also inevitably reclaims those who were there, and so if you are a veteran, I urge you to do as my father has done here and write down your own story to share with others, especially for your family and for other people in the Armed Services who can learn from your example.

If you are a family member of a veteran of WWII, or any era, get them to understand again the value of their experiences. Get them to step on this path; get them—for the sake of those who will come after—to take this journey again.

Appendix

Military Service
Proposed citation—Fort Lewis
Letter of Recommendation for Promotion
Honorable Title—SAS DC-8 Royal Viking Airline
Certificate of Achievement—Yakima, Washington
Certificates of Completion
Military Leadership—Fort Benning, Georgia
Unit and Organization Supply—Fort Lee, Virginia
Training and Methods of Instruction—Fort Benning, Georgia
Commissary Operation—Fort Lee
Quartermaster Company Extended Courses—Fort Benning, Georgia
Personnel Management—Fort Benning
Commendation and Appreciation Letter—Fort Lewis
Certificate of Achievement—Fort Lewis
Certificate of Achievement—Sixth U.S. Army
Army Commendation Medal Fourth Infantry Division, Fort Lewis
Letter of Recommendation—Fort Lewis
Recommendation for Award—Fourth Infantry Division Trains
Recommendation for Award—Fort Lewis
President Truman Thank You
Army Commendation Medal—Fort Lewis
Combat Infantry Badge—1944
Certificate of Training—370 Armored Infantry Battalion, Munich, Germany
Civilian Life
System Manager Food Service—Northwest Orient
Department of Foreign Carrier Appreciation
Highly Commendable Six-Year Employee Report—Northwest Airlines
Five-Year Recognition Pin—Northwest Airlines
Certificate of Achievement—U.S. Army of Alaska 1994,1995
Outstanding Service—U.S. Army of Alaska 1996
Certificate of Appreciation—Department of the Army, Fort Richardson, Alaska
Mayor's Award for Public Service—Anchorage, Alaska
U.S. Chamber of Commerce Board of Directors Election
Board and Commission Member—Parking Authority, Municipality of Anchorage

HEADQUARTERS
4TH INFANTRY DIVISION TRAINS
Fort Lewis, Washington

15 June 1963

SUBJECT: Letter of Recommendation

TO WHOM IT MAY CONCERN:

1. Within two weeks SFC Ollen Hunt, RA 37 399 586, will be retiring from the Army after more than 20 years of honorable, active military service. SFC Hunt has been the Mess Sergeant of Headquarters Division Trains during my six months in command.

2. I have the highest regard for SFC Hunt as a food service administrator and producer. The Mess operated by SFC Hunt is considered by many the best in the 4th Infantry Division. In addition to his exceptional ability in food preparation and serving, he is a capable administrator and has served as Unit First Sergeant and Orderly of the Unit Fund.

3. I recommend SFC Hunt without qualification as a welcome addition to any civilian enterprise with which he becomes associated.

UERIN
y

HEADQUARTERS DETACHMENT & BAND
4th Infantry Division Trains
Fort Lewis, Washington

4 March 1962

SUBJECT: Letter of Commendation and Appreciation

TO: Sergeant First Class (E6) Ollen Hunt, RA 37 399 586
        Headquarters & Headquarters Detachment
        4th Infantry Division Trains
        Fort Lewis, Washington

1. Upon the termination of my active duty status and departure from this unit, I especially desire to express to you my appreciation for the outstanding performance of duty which you have rendered and which I have observed since 19 December 1958, the date of my arrival.

2. During my more than twenty years service, I have not witnessed nor have I known a more loyal and devoted soldier. Your dedication to the Army is the most complete and selfless it has been my privilege to encounter. Your constructive influence has instilled into the men of this detachment principles of character and moral traits which added to every man's maturity and development and I was always both proud and grateful for your presence in the unit.

3. In your TOE assignment as Mess Steward for the Detachment and Band, your accomplishments were exemplary. The demonstrated proficiency, both technical and functional, of the mess operations in the field denotes a professional ability unique in a specialized field.

4. The performance of your additional duties as First Sergeant while in the garrison status emphasized the versatility with which you are so fortunately endowed. The wholesome and intelligent manner of your approach to all missions of the unit inspired confidence in our success. You have consistently displayed the finest qualities of the military man and I shall always remember you as the most admirable noncommissioned officer I have ever known.

FRED L. IMMES
Major, Inf
Commanding

155

HEADQUARTERS 4TH INFANTRY DIVISION TRAINS
Fort Lewis, Washington

18 March 1960

SUBJECT: Letter of Commendation and Appreciation

TO: Sergeant First Class Ollen Hunt, RA37399586
        Headquarters Detachment, 4th Inf Div Trains
        Fort Lewis, Washington

1. Upon my departure from the 4th Infantry Division Trains I would like to commend you for the outstanding manner in which you performed your duties as Mess Steward and Assistant First Sergeant for the Trains Headquarters. Both in garrison and in the field your efficient and confident approach to every task achieved superior results. In the major exercises INDIAN RIVER and DRY HILLS, and numerous Command Post Exercises, the Division Trains Headquarters mess under your management and supervision was constantly outstanding. Without exception, all meals were appetizing, nourishing, attractively served and enjoyed by all personnel messing with our headquarters.

2. The conversion from garrison duties of that of Assistant First Sergeant to Mess Steward in the field was expertly accomplished. The Headquarters mess personnel under your supervision demonstrated the highest degree of professional competence in practicing correct tactical measures while concurrently providing superior and timely meals.

3. Especially noteworthy was the splendid military bearing, courteous attitude and careful appearance which characterized your daily presence. Your influence on the personnel of the headquarters detachment and your associates endowed them with traits of esprit and loyalty which will tend to serve each of them well. I wish for you continued success in all of your endeavours. Your loyal and steadfast support has been deeply appreciated.

EDWARD S. BERRY

ARMY COMMENDATION MEDAL

CITATION

SERGEANT FIRST CLASS (E-6) OLLEN HUNT, RA 37 399 586, Headquarters Detachment, 4th Infantry Division Trains, is cited for meritorious service as Mess Steward, during the period 16 August 1957 to 31 July 1963. While serving in this capacity, Sergeant Hunt exhibited the highest degree of professional knowledge and ability in the operation and maintainence of any mess under his supervision. His tireless efforts were responsible for the superior standards of food preparation, mess sanitation, and personnel utilization being maintained in his mess hall. In every inspection, his mess section received the highest rating possible. In the field, Sergeant Hunt provided outstanding service for as many as one hundred and fifty men, with a staff intended by TO&E to serve sixty men. His field mess has been consistently commended by visiting commanders and senior staff officers as the "best mess in the 4th Infantry Division". The extra, personal effort of Sergeant Hunt contributed materially to the high state of morale found in his unit. Also during this period, Sergeant Hunt served approximately two years as Headquarters Detachment First Sergeant, and for the past three years as Recorder of the unit fund. These responsibilities, as all his other duties, have been performed in a highly exemplary manner. Sergeant Hunt's leadership, professional ability and devotion to duty have earned for him the respect and admiration of all and reflect great credit upon himself and the United States Army.

Chamber of Commerce of the United States of America

*By invitation, and having been duly elected
by the Chambers Board of Directors*

Hof Brau

*is a Business Member of the
Chamber of Commerce
of the United States of America*

September 1986

Richard L Lesher

President

UNITED STATES ARMY ALASKA

CERTIFICATE OF ACHIEVEMENT

is awarded on this   25th   day of   April   , 1995

to

SFC (Ret) Ollen Hunt

for

OUTSTANDING SERVICE TO THE COMMUNITY. YOUR CONTRIBUTION AS A DEDICATED VOLUNTEER HAS BEEN AN INVALUABLE ASSET TO OUR COMMUNITY. YOUR UNSELFISH SERVICE HAS ADDED SIGNIFICANTLY TO THE ENHANCEMENT OF THE QUALITY OF LIFE OF SOLDIERS, FAMILY MEMBERS, RETIREES, AND CIVILIAN EMPLOYEES ON THIS INSTALLATION AND REFLECTS GREAT CREDIT UPON YOURSELF, YOUR FAMILY, AND OUR COMMUNITY.

US Army Alaska Retiree Council

Thomas H. Needham
THOMAS H. NEEDHAM
MAJOR GENERAL, USA
COMMANDING

USARAK Form 873, 1 Oct 94

Anchorage

Municipality of Anchorage

P.O. BOX 196650
ANCHORAGE, ALASKA 99519-6650
TELEPHONE: (907) 343-4431
FAX: (907) 272-1991

Tom Fink, Mayor

OFFICE OF THE MAYOR

November 10, 1992

Mr. Ollen Hunt
Hof Brau Restaurant
Anchorage, Alaska 99501

Dear Mr. Hunt:

On behalf of the residents of the Municipality of Anchorage, I want to thank you for your service on the Anchorage Parking Authority Board of Directors. Giving of personal time and effort to public service always demands a bit of sacrifice, and I appreciate your making that sacrifice.

To have persons such as you provide advice and counsel to government is important to the process of democracy. I appreciate your service to the Municipality, and I wish you success in your future endeavors.

Enclosed is a Public Service Award in recognition of your service.

Sincerely,

Tom Fink

Enclosure

cc: Dave Harbour
     Jane Ferguson

Municipality of Anchorage

P.O. BOX 196650
ANCHORAGE, ALASKA 99519-6650
(907) 343-4431

TOM FINK,
MAYOR

OFFICE OF THE MAYOR

March 30, 1990

Mr. Ollen Hunt
414 W. 6th Avenue
Anchorage, Alaska 99501

Dear Mr. Hunt:

I would like to inform you that the Assembly has now confirmed your reappointment to the Anchorage Parking Authority. The term expires February 14, 1993.

Congratulations! I am pleased to have you share with me in the process of local government. Your advice and counsel through your participation as a commission member are a significant part of representative government.

Board and commission members may purchase comprehensive health insurance through the Municipality's group plan, and they are also eligible for membership in the Alaskan Federal Credit Union. Specific information on these two options which are open to you may be acquired by calling our Employee Relations Department at 343-6882.

In order to comply with the Municipal Code of Ethics (Section 1.15.200), it will be necessary for you to complete the enclosed "Conflict of Interest" form and return it to the Municipal Clerk's office.

Henry Pratt is my staff manager for boards and commissions, and you can reach him at 343-4410 if you have any questions or suggestions.

Again my congratulations.

Sincerely,

Tom Fink

Enclosure

cc: Dave Harbour
     Pam Amstrup, Records and Benefits
     Ruby Veldkamp, Municipal Clerk

THE **Odom** CORPORATION

June 10, 2002

Ref: Mr. Ollen Hunt

To Whom It May Concern:

I have known Ollen Hunt for 33 years. For most of those years, I have considered him a personal friend. He is a very honest and kind individual. Mr. Hunt is a family man, active in his church and church organizations. He is a big supporter of the youth of our community offering help and advise when called upon.

Our Company had very honorable business dealings with Mr. Hunt for a number of years when he owned and operated the Hof Brau Restaurant in Anchorage. He has been an active member of the Anchorage Downtown Merchants Association for a number of years.

Sincerely,

James R. Odom

James R. Odom
Senior Vice President

Mayor's Award for Public Service

On behalf of the good people of the
Municipality of Anchorage,
it is with great pleasure that I honor

Ollen Hunt

with this citation for

his outstanding contribution to the community as a member of the Anchorage Parking Authority

11/10/92
DATE

Tom Fink
MAYOR TOM FINK

Municipality of Anchorage

245 West 5th Ave., Suite 124
Anchorage, Alaska 99501
ph 907-279-5650 fax 907-279-5651
email: ancdp@alaska.net

ANCHORAGE
DOWNTOWN
PARTNERSHIP

Dear Ollen:

I would like to thank you for your support of the Anchorage Downtown Partnership as a member of the Board of Directors, by getting the most new members in 2000, helping the youth in service, and always being interested in downtown and a clean, safe, and vital community.

The help that you have provided to the downtown community is priceless and you are greatly missed. You are a great example to youth at what it takes to work hard and how to respect the people, young and old, in your life.

Thank you for having such a great heart in wanting your community to be safe and friendly. Your hard work is very appreciated. I hope that wherever life takes you that you are truly happy and successful.

Sincerely,

Rod Pfleiger
Executive Director